*A comprehensive guide*
*to the diction of*
*Italian, Ecclesiastical Latin,*
*French and German*
*with practical exercises*
*in a comparative approach*
*for American singers*

Italian Latin French German
...the sounds and 81 exercises for

E.C. Schirmer Music Company

singing them

John Moriarty

# Diction

Boston, Massachusetts

Designed and edited by Thomas Dunn
Graphic production by William S. Thorpe

# FOREWORD

Most of us who call ourselves singers have had, at one time or another, a dream in which a mythical being descends from above—as in Baroque opera—and imparts to us instantly and painlessly the knowledge possessed by a linguistic scholar. Most of us awaken, smiling, and then proceed to our study of diction, frowning.

Herein, three common hazards to singers (Italian, French and German) are dealt with in concise terms, using the standard international phonetic alphabet, and are made lucid by a thorough comparison to equivalent sounds in English. Even the simplest among us cannot but benefit from the serious application of this amassment of material.

My only regret is that so many of us had to learn the hard and long way what is available here.

**Margaret Harshaw**
Professor of Voice at the University of Indiana

## EDITOR'S NOTE

The text runs continuously on right pages in Part 1. When an exercise is indicated, it will be found on the facing left page. All references to exercises are given in bold-face type, both in the indices to the several languages spread throughout Part 2 and in the general index at the end of the book.

# PREFACE TO THE SECOND EDITION

The first edition of this book was put together primarily for use in my diction classes at the New England Conservatory. It was not intended to be used independently. Consequently much detail was omitted, to be filled in during class and drill sessions. The widespread interest evinced by singers, teachers, schools and professional organizations has indicated that a more complete version could be of practical use. Hence this new edition.

Part 1 describes the physical factors in the production of vowel and consonant sounds in the four languages. 81 exercises are included covering all phases of the text, complementing the rules of pronunciation set forth in Part 2 language by language. A beneficial way of using the text, therefore, would be the alternation of the rules of Part 2 with the appropriate exercises of Part 1.

Much of the material in Part 2 is unchanged from the original edition. Some has been expanded. Since its publication in 1969 I have found a more effective order or manner of presentation of some of the material. Sometimes students have devised ingenious short cuts which I have been hasty to incorporate into the text. To them I acknowledge indebtedness.

Thanks are also due to Mark Pearson, Barbara Reutlinger, Nadine Harris and Anna Yona, all of the Conservatory faculty, and Elizabeth Boehme and Paul Laplante of Northeastern University for their assistance and invaluable suggestions.

**J.M.** Boston, 1973

*vii*

## TABLE OF CONTENTS

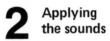

**2** **Applying
the sounds**

# INTRODUCTION

The American singer who desires a career in opera has to be able to act, perhaps dance, look like a movie star, and sing expertly in at least four languages. The singer who aspires to a career on the concert stage must have at his command at least four or five languages, and is expected to pronounce them with even more refinement and skill than his operatic colleagues. The task of developing such language skill seems enormous; difficult it is, but not impossible.

Speaking a foreign language is difficult because of problems of intonation, stress and cadence. Singers have most of these problems solved for them in advance by composers, who determine where the voice rises and falls, how long the syllables are, where pauses occur, and even where the stresses fall. But the singer is faced with a situation that the speaker can often slur over: he must sustain each vowel and consonant sound to satisfy the most careful listening. It becomes, for example, a matter of major importance whether the vowel is pronounced **aw** or [o], or as the English diphthong **o-oo** when it occurs as the first syllable of *Ombra mai fu*, held for four slow beats. At such times accuracy of pronounciation becomes tremendously significant.

All singers must study diction. But American singers, because their speech tends to be quite imprecise, in particular need to make a thorough study of phonetics and diction. Our vowels are vague and often back-produced. We tend to make diphthongs out of monophthongs, triphthongs of diphthongs. Our consonants are carelessly produced, often imploded, almost never clearly articulated, and the strong tonic stress of our language encourages us to slur over unstressed syllables. We practice bad diction in nearly every utterance.

American singers striving for good diction often erroneously believe that the solution to their problems can be found in a highly explosive production of consonants. While it is true that the consonants must be articulated more clearly in singing than in the usual sloppy speech of every day, just as important for the singer (perhaps more so) is the production of clear and easily identified vowels.

Accuracy and clarity in pronunciation are the subjects of this book. But they are only first steps in the establishment of authentic style in language. Capturing the flavor and subtle colors is a skill resulting from long study of singers singing their native language. And the flavor and color are not the only benefits of accurate pronunciation: often vocal production makes a startling and immediate improvement when the articulation of vowels and consonants becomes clear. Diction might be called the orchestration of singing, and far too many singers neglect the wide range of possibilities for color found in the spectrum of vowel and consonant sounds.

The symbols used throughout this book are those of the International Phonetic Association. Singers who grumble at having to learn another alphabet may soon find the symbols a remarkably economical short-hand, useful in self-reminding, and an aid in teaching once a sound has been associated with its symbol. For, while spelling varies greatly from language to language, a symbol always represents one sound—a help in assisting singers in using the many excellent pronouncing dictionaries now available.

The multi-lingual approach to diction set out in this book was first developed in classes attended by Apprentice Artists at the Santa Fe Opera. It has been developed further at the New England Conservatory. It proceeds from American English, compares the vowel and consonant sounds of Italian, French, German and Ecclesiastical Latin with each other and relates them to sounds spoken in the United States. All too often foreign-born language teachers, lacking a clear understanding of English, have been unable to draw useful or even accurate parallels and find themselves in the position of the Russian teacher who, in describing the Russian dark **l**, said that it was like the **l** in the English word **lead**, unaware that such a sound could only occur if the English word were pronounced with a heavy Russian accent.

Those wishing to pursue more intensive study will find Ralph Errolle's **Italian Diction for Singers** excellent as are Madeleine Marshall's **Singers Manual of English Diction**, Sieb's **Deutsche Hochsprache**, and Fouché's **Traité de la prononciation française**, whose many footnotes point out the differences between conversational style and *le style soutenu*.

**J.M.**
Boston, 1969

*To my students*

*When first I considered my diction*
*I knew my Italian was fiction.*
*But this year I know*
*How to round a closed* [o]
*And open* [ɛ] *causes no friction.*
                                    **SPHS**

# 1 Forming and practicing the sounds

## VOWEL CLASSIFICATION

*What are vowels?*   In his book **The Sounds of English and German**
William G. Moulton defines them as "sounds articulated in such a
way that the breath stream flows essentially unhindered along the
median line of the vocal tract." The vocal cords are in vibration.
Consonants, on the other hand, are produced either by a partial
obstruction of the breath stream (as with **l** or **v**), or by a total obstruction followed by an expulsion of air (as with **t** or **p**). The vocal
cords may or may not be in vibration, according to the consonant.

The continuous, unobstructed stream of breath may be shaped
in two ways to produce vowels and to give them identity:
1. by varying the height of the tongue (compare English
   **me** and **met**)
2. by varying the position of the lips (compare English
   **moo** and **ma**)

The Italian name for vowel is **vocale**. We may infer from this
name that clear, accurate, effortlessly produced vowels are the basis
of singing, that they carry the timbre of the voice and the musical
line. They are also the basis of good diction. In singing, much more
time is spent on vowels than on consonants, whether the word be
**love**, **Liebe**, **amour** or **amore**.

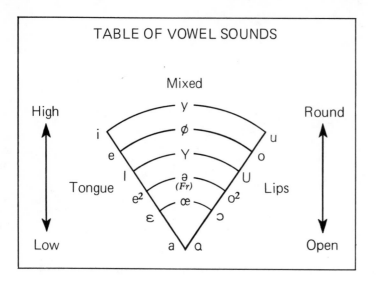

TABLE OF VOWEL SOUNDS

Mixed

High     Round

Tongue     Lips

Low     Open

*Vowel classification*

Most phoneticists classify vowels in three groups: frontal, central and back. These terms refer to the position of the tongue. For example, in the English **me** the vowel would be frontal, in **ma** it would be central, and in **moo** it would be back.

The word "back", however, is anathema to many singers and teachers of singing. For this and additional reasons, we find it more useful to classify the vowels in five groups as *tongue vowels, lip vowels* (according to which factor is most active in their formation), *mixed vowels, neutral vowels* and *nasalized vowels*.

## FORMING VOWELS

**Tongue vowels**   Smile and say English **me** and **met**. The first vowel, spelled
                    variously as **ee** in **seek**, **ea** in **feat**, **ei** in **receive**, **ie** in **chief**, etc., has
         [i]        the phonetic designation [i]. When it is pronounced, the center of
         [ε]        the tongue has a higher position than for the vowel in **met** [ε]. The
                    tongue is closer to the roof of the mouth and the space between is
                    partially closed.  The adjective "closed" is often applied to this
                    vowel.  Since the term "closed vowel" can be wrongly equated with
                    "closed throat", the unfortunate connotations will be avoided by
                    the designation "high vowel".

                    It is possible to pronounce the vowel [i] without smiling.  In-
                    structions here and below about smiling, puckering lips, etc., are
                    given for the purpose of leading the singer to the easiest way of
                    making accurate vowel sounds, all of which can be pronounced
                    with a variety of facial expressions.

         [I]        Now say the vowel [i] and, continuing the sound, gradually
                    lower the tongue and jaw into the position for [ε]. You will
                    notice that on the way from [i] to [ε], there are numerous stopping
                    places for possible vowels.  About half-way between [i] and [ε] is
                    the position for the vowel [I], which occurs in English **mitt**.  Now
                    alternate **mitt** and **me**, and the vowels [I] — [i] — [I] — [i] to feel
                    the changing tongue positions.  Then try [i] — [I] — [ε] — [I] — [i].

*9*

# 1

*Practice saying and singing the following series of vowels:*

[i] - [e] - [I] - [ɛ]  *and*  [ɛ] - [I] - [e] - [i]

# 2

*Practice saying and singing:*

[i] - [e] - [I] - [e²] - [ɛ]  *and*  [ɛ] - [e²] - [I] - [e] -[i]

# 3

*Practice saying and singing the tongue vowels in succession,
from top to bottom and from bottom to top. Keep the lips relaxed
in a smiling position. Although you will find the smile a little
broader for the lower vowels, the lips do not play an important
role in this vowel series.*

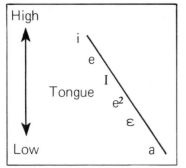

[e]    Approximately half-way between the tongue positions of [I] and [i] is a vowel which is quite common in French and German, but which does not really exist as a sustained vowel sound in standard English. This is [e] (closed **e**). It occurs in French in words like **bébé** and in German in words like **Beet**.

*Exercise 1*

In the previous exercise the change in the height of the tongue should be very slight between [i] and [e] or [e] and [I]. From [I] to [ɛ], however, you should find a marked drop in tongue and jaw.

[e²]    About half-way between [I] and [ɛ] is still another vowel. It occurs in Italian in words like **vero**, and in German in words like **Tränen** and is also known as a "closed" **e** (high **e**), even though it is not nearly as closed (high) as [e], or even [I]. We shall give it the designation [e²]. It occurs in English as the first vowel sound in **chaotic**, and is also heard in **day** if it is pronounced with an Irish brogue. Natives of the American northern mid-west (Wisconsin, Minnesota, Illinois, etc.) will tend to pronounce **chaotic** with [e] rather than with [e²].

*Exercise 2*

[a]    If you continue lowering the tongue and jaw, keeping a smile, you will find the French vowel [a] occuring five times in the phrase **Voilà la salade!**

*Exercise 3*

# 4

*Practice saying and singing:*

[u] - [ɔ]  *and*  [ɔ] - [u]

*It is important to start the first vowel with well rounded lips and a loose, lightly dropped jaw. Otherwise a throaty vowel, common in careless or colloquial speech, will result.*

# 5

*Practice saying and singing:*

[u] - [U] - [ɔ]  *and* [ɔ] - [U] - [u]

[u]    With well-rounded, projecting lips and a slightly dropped jaw,
[ɔ]    say English **boon** and then English **bought**. It will be found that
in the second word the rounded position of the lips has given way to
a vertical oval, that there is less closure of the lips, and that the jaw
has dropped somewhat more. We may say that the first vowel is
more "closed" ("round" is a more useful term) than the second. The
phonetic symbol for the vowel in **boon** is [u] ; in **bought** (in standard
English) [ɔ]. Natives of the southern and mid-western United States
often pronounce the [ɔ] vowel differently. Correct formation of
this vowel is discussed further on pages 45-47.

*Exercise 4*

As with the tongue series, if you start with [u] and gradually change
to [ɔ], you will find many possible intermediate stopping places
where other vowels may be found.

[U]    Midway between [u] and [ɔ] is the vowel [U], as in English **look**.
The lips should still be rather rounded and protruding for producing
this vowel in singing. Do not allow the lips to form a horizontal oval
for this vowel or it will be throaty and unpleasant.

*Exercise 5*

13

# 6

*Practice saying and singing:*

[u] - [o] - [U] - [ɔ]  *and*  [ɔ] - [U] - [o] - [u]

# 7

*Practice saying and singing:*

[u] - [o] - [U] - [o²] - [ɔ]

*Start with well-rounded lips (puckered position) and with a relaxed
and slightly dropped jaw. As you progress through the series to [ɔ],
you should feel the jaw dropping. Simultaneously the roundness
should finally give way to a vertical oval. Keep the tongue
relaxed with its tip resting against the back of the lower teeth.
By the time you reach [ɔ], the corners of the mouth should
still be slightly held in gently towards center.
Be sure to practice the series in reverse order.*

# 8

*Practice saying and singing the lip vowels in succession, from
top to bottom and bottom to top.*

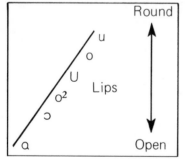

[o]    Midway between [u] and [U] is a vowel sometimes known as "closed"
       **o**, which we shall call "round" **o**. Its phonetic symbol is [o]. Like
       [e], it does not really exist in English, but does occur in French **beau**
       and German **Boot**.

*Exercise 6*

[o²]   As with the tongue series, there should be very little change in po-
       sition between the first and second, and the second and third vowels.
       But a marked difference in lip formation should occur between [U]
       and [ɔ]. Between them is another "closed" **o**, not nearly so closed
       (round) as the vowel [o]. We shall designate it [o²]. It occurs in
       Italian words like **nome** and **voce**, and in English as the first vowel
       in **rowing**. It may also be heard in **go** if pronounced with an Irish
       brogue.

*Exercise 7*

[ɑ]    If the corners of the mouth are relaxed completely, [ɑ], the lowest
       vowel of all emerges. Do not draw the corners of the mouth into
       a smile; that will produce the French vowel [a].

*Exercise 8*

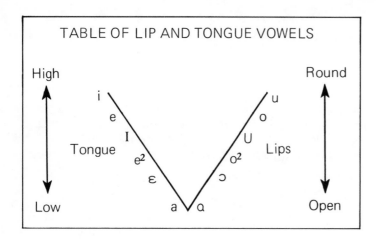

TABLE OF LIP AND TONGUE VOWELS

It will be seen from the diagram opposite that [i] and [e] on the tongue side have the same relationship to each other that [u] and [o] have to each other on the lip side. In each pair the vowels are closely related to each other in formation, and therefore quite similar in sound. The only difference between [i] and [e] is the ever so slightly lower position of the tongue for the second vowel, which is more open.

Singers sometimes say that they cannot sing the proper vowel in the first syllable of German **leben** because it is too closed. Yet the same singers often have no difficulty with **lieben** [li bən], even though the vowel in the first syllable is even more closed. Much of the difficulty comes from the terminology (*closed* is a bad word), lack of understanding of phonetic principles, or old wives' tales about "closed vowels". Anyone who can sing **lieben** should be able to sing **leben** more easily because its first vowel is the more open.

It is sometimes helpful to think of these vowels [i] and [e] as "high" and "less high". A parallel in French is found in the words **ni** [ni] and **né** [ne].

On the other side of the diagram, [u] and [o] are similar in formation and sound. Anyone who can sing the French **fou** can sing **faut** [fo] with the proper vowel sound, perhaps more easily because it is slightly more open (less round). A German parallel can be found in **Ruh** [ru] and **roh** [ro].

# 9

*Practice saying and singing:*

| | | |
|---|---|---|
| [i] | [u] | [y] |
| [e] | [o] | [ø] |
| [ɛ] | [ɔ] | [œ] |
| [y] | [ø] | [œ] |
| [œ] | [ø] | [y] |

# 10

*Practice saying and singing the mixed vowels from top to bottom and from bottom to top. Be sure that the lip and tongue positions of each vowel are accurate.*

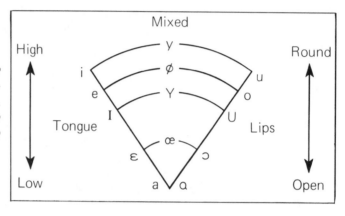

# 11

*Because mixed vowels are unfamiliar to English-speaking singers, it is necessary to train tongue and lips to find them easily and naturally. First make the correct vowels in speech. Then sing them on a pitch. Avoid unnecessary tension in lips, jaw and tongue. Next sing a scale. Devise little vocal exercises so that you discover how these vowels feel when you sing them in different parts of your vocal range.*

[u]  +  [i]  =  [y]          [o]  +  [e]  =  [ø]

[U]  +  [I]  =  [Y]          [ɔ]  +  [ɛ]  =  [œ]

[y]   French and German have a third category of vowels. They
are called *mixed* because they employ the tongue position of one
vowel simultaneously with the lip position of another. If, for example,
you shape your lips for [u] and say [i], you will form a vowel which
exists in German **früh** and French **fut**. Its phonetic symbol is [y].

[ø]   If you shape your lips for [o] and say [e], you will sound the
vowel in the German **schön** and the French **feu**. Its phonetic symbol is [ø].

[œ]   Shape the lips for [ɔ] and pronounce [ɛ]. The resultant vowel [œ]
is in the German **könnt** and the French **coeur.**

*Exercise 9*

It will be found in the succession [y]-[ø]-[œ] that there is only a
slight change in position between the first two vowels. This is to be
expected because the change of position from [i] to [e] and from
[u] to [o] is very slight. From [ø] to [œ], however, there is a
marked drop of the jaw and unrounding of the lips. Here again an
intermediate vowel is found.

[Y]   Shape the lips for [U] and say [I]. The resulting vowel exists in
German, as in **Glück**, but does not exist in French. The phonetic
designation for this vowel is [Y]. It is higher and rounder than [œ],
but not as high and round as [ø].

*Exercise 10*

None of these mixed vowels exists either in English or in Italian.
Sometimes teachers try to be helpful by saying that the vowel [ø]
somewhat resembles the vowel in the English **her**. Nothing could
be more misleading. The vowel in **her** [3] has a much less rounded lip
position and a lower tongue position.

*Exercise 11*

19

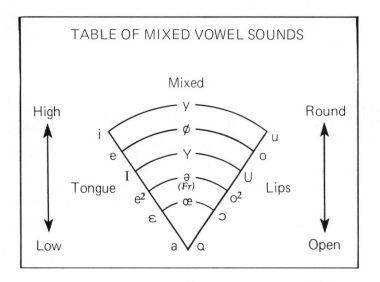

TABLE OF MIXED VOWEL SOUNDS

[ə]   Many languages possess a neutral vowel (sometimes known as *schwa*) which is used in certain unstressed positions in words. Its phonetic designation is [ə].

The final vowel sound in each of the English words **metal**, **heaven**, **handsome**, **murmur**, **foreign**, **ocean** is a neutral vowel. It is a vague, elusive sound because it is unstressed and is passed over rapidly in speech. In the sustained diction of singing, the neutral vowel often has to be prolonged to an extent unnatural in speech.

Most phonetic symbols stand for a sound more or less similar in all languages. [ɛ] is the symbol for the vowel in **bed** (Eng.), **bello** (It.), **belle** (Fr.) **Bett** (Ger.). [i] is the vowel in **see** (Eng.), **sieh'** (Ger.), **si** (Fr.) and **si** (It.). The symbol [ə], however, does not stand so much for a specific vowel as for a concept: a vague, neutral sound. The actual sound of the vowel varies from language to language and depends on the general placement or positioning of the language. French is a very forward-placed language; consequently, the neutral vowel also sounds forward. English tends to be a rather back-placed language, so its neutral is much darker than in French. German finds its center somewhere between these two, but closer to English. Standard Italian has no neutral vowel, although some Italian dialects do.

The French [ə] is possibly the easiest to find because it actually is another mixed vowel. Find the lip position of [o²]. (Jaw dropped, lips relaxed and somewhat rounded in a pout, the corners of the mouth also relaxed and drawn in slightly.) Now with the lip position of [o²] say [e²]. The resulting vowel is the French [ə], such as in **je** or at the end of **rose**. On the vowel chart we would find it between [Y] and [œ].

The German and English neutrals [ə] do not employ any rounding or projection of the lips. Say English **the** unemphatically. Now say it with the French [ə] in order to contrast the different sounds. Not only do the English and German neutrals avoid a rounding of the lips, they are also pronounced with a slight depression of the center of the

# 12

*Contrast the vowels in the following words:*

| *French* [ə] | *German* [ə] | *English* [ə] | *English* [ʌ] |
|---|---|---|---|
| le | (See)len | (A)lan | lung |
| te | (be)ten | (Sa)tan | ton |
| de | (re)den | (la)den | done |
| me | (ar)men | (lay)man | munch |

[ʌ]   tongue. Now contrast **the**, or better still the second syllable of **oven**, with English **but**.  The vowel in **but** is stressed [ʌ], pronounced with a lower jaw and a trench down the center of the tongue deeper than in the vowel of **the** or **oven**.  Both vowels may be heard in English **butted** [bʌ təd] .

English-speaking singers often make an erroneous substitution of the vowel [ʌ] for the true neutral vowels of French and German. Such a substitution is, of course, to be avoided.  The vowel [ʌ], as in English **thus**, **must**, **but**, **dust**, etc., does not exist in French, German or Italian.

German [ə]   If the center-tongue depression is eliminated completely from the word **but**, the resulting vowel is the German neutral, neither as dark as [ʌ], nor as bright as the French [ə].  This elimination is accomplished by merely relaxing the tongue.  The German [ə] should feel completely relaxed and central — truly neutral.

*Exercise 12*

When practicing the sound of [ə] in German and English, prolong the vowel unnaturally, as it might be in a musical setting.  Consider the length of the second vowel in **sinkest** and **nieder** in the Schubert song **Nacht und Träume**.  Take care, however, that you do not fall into substituting the English vowel [ʌ]; this will happen if you drop the jaw too far, or if there is a depression down the center of your tongue.

It should be repeated here that the detailed instructions about position of tongue, lips, jaw, etc., are for the purpose of leading the singer to a discovery of the authentic vowel sounds.  After they have been securely established, the singer will perhaps wish to put less emphasis on the purely physical aspects of these vowel formations, and will wish to adapt the formations to his method of vocal production. If the production is at all honest, it should be possible to effect this adaptation without sacrificing the identity of the vowels.

*23*

# 13

*Practice saying and singing the following words in succession, reading from left to right. Smile and keep the jaw and tongue relaxed, with the tip of the tongue resting against the back of the lower teeth. When saying the German and French words, let the center of the tongue find its higher position. Be sure to maintain the same vowel sound throughout the duration of the German and French vowels. Do not lock or freeze the tongue in place; rather let it stay in place in a relaxed manner.*

| *English* [Ii] | *German* [i] | | *French* [i] | |
|----------------|--------------|--------|--------------|----------|
| see  | **sieht** | [zit]  | **ici**  | [i si]  |
| dean | **dien**  | [din]  | **dîne** | [di nə] |
| veep | **Wien**  | [vin]  | **vie**  | [vi ə]  |
| fee  | **Vieh**  | [fi]   | **fit**  | [fi]    |

# 14

*Pay careful attention to the consistency of the French and German vowels. A consonant should not affect the sound of the vowel preceding it. Consonants must be executed quickly and cleanly. In singing, do not allow German **wir** to sound like* [viər] *or* [vi ə].

| *English* | *German* | | *French* | |
|-----------|----------|--------|----------|----------|
| veer  | **wir**   | [vir]  | **vie**   | [vi ə]   |
| mere  | **mir**   | [mir]  | **mie**   | [mi ə]   |
| ear   | **ihr**   | [ir]   | **irise** | [i ri zə]|
| dear  | **dir**   | [dir]  | **dire**  | [di rə]  |
| lease | **liess** | [lis]  | **lys**   | [lis]    |

# COMPARING ITALIAN, FRENCH AND GERMAN VOWELS

**Tongue vowels**  The vowel [i] has exactly the same sound in French and German.
**[i]**  The Italian vowel is slightly different, and the American vowel is
markedly different.

Let the tip of the tongue rest against the back of the lower
teeth.  Now smile and pronounce English **me**, prolonging the vowel
so that you can investigate its formation.  You will find that the
tongue humps up, about half-way back in the mouth.  This makes
the closure, or height, giving the vowel its identity.  If you say the
word quickly, you will also find that the tongue rises still higher
at the conclusion of the vowel sound.  This extra movement, however slight, produces what is known as an off-glide or diphthong glide.

[i] is a diphthong in normal American speech, although not as
obvious as the diphthong in **my** or **boy**.  It could be notated with
phonetic symbols [Ii].  This diphthong glide does not occur in the
German, French or Italian [i].  In those languages  the vowel keeps
exactly the same formation and therefore the same sound  from
beginning to end.  The high tongue position at the end of the English
diphthong [Ii] is actually the tongue position of the French and
German [i].

*Exercises 13 and 14*

25

# 15

*Contrast the following:*

| English | Italian | | French | |
|---------|---------|------|--------|------|
| me | mi | [mi] | mie | [mi] |
| see | si | [si] | ici | [i si] |
| tea | ti | [ti] | tire | [ti rə] |
| dee *(letter)* | di | [di] | dire | [di rə] |
| jeer | gira | [dʒi ra] | gît | [ʒi] |
| tear | tira | [ti ra] | tire | [ti rə] |

# 16

*Practice saying and singing the following in German, reading from left to right. Both vowels should feel alike in production.*

| [i] | | [e] | |
|-----|------|-----|------|
| wir | [vir] | wer | [ver] |
| mir | [mir] | mehr | [mer] |
| hier | [hir] | her | [her] |
| ihr | [ir] | er | [er] |
| dir | [dir] | der | [der] |
| Bier | [bir] | Behr | [ber] |
| lieben | [li bən] | leben | [le bən] |
| siegen | [zi gən] | Segen | [ze gən] |

# 17

*Try saying and singing the following French words. Stay relaxed and avoid grimaces. Do not allow the tone to sound pinched when singing* [e].

| [i] | | [e] | |
|-----|------|-----|------|
| j'y | [ʒi] | j'ai | [ʒe] |
| nid | [ni] | nez | [ne] |
| qui | [ki] | quai | [ke] |
| dis | [di] | dé | [de] |
| habit | [a bi] | abbé | [a be] |

# 18

*Sing the following French and German words. The vowels should match. Avoid any off-glides in the French. In the German do not anticipate the formation of any consonants occurring after* [e].

| French | | German | |
|--------|------|--------|------|
| nez | [ne] | neben | [ne bən] |
| dé | [de] | Demut | [de mut] |
| mé | [me] | Meer | [mer] |
| abbé | [a be] | Beet | [bet] |
| allez | [a le] | leben | [le bən] |
| café | [ka fe] | fehlen | [fe lən] |

*Tongue vowels*
[i] [e]

The tongue position for Italian [i] is neither as high as the French-German vowel, nor as low as the beginning of the English vowel. The Italian vowel has no diphthong glide. The French-German vowel is made with more of a smile then the Italian vowel.

Note: Throughout this book, no indications will be given for vowel quantity (long and short), because vowel length, in singing is dependent on the length of the musical note. Thus, a word like **sieht** in German, commonly notated [zi:t] in dictionaries, will appear here simply as [zit].

The Langenscheidt Dictionary uses the symbol [i] where this manual uses [I] to indicate the open vowel. It uses [i:] where this manual uses [i] for the closed vowel.

*Exercise 15*

[e]   The vowel [e] has no direct counterpart in English. It is a very high vowel, nearly as high as [i]. Many American singers do not form [i] high enough. As a consequence, they have difficulty distinguishing between [i] and [e].

Relax the jaw and lips. Let the tip of the tongue rest against the back of the lower teeth. Smile and pronounce [i] as it sounds in German and French, with a rather high arching of the central part of the tongue. Now let this arching relax down slightly. You should have sounded [e].

*Exercise 16*

To sing [e], use the same approach as for [i]. Think of [e] as [i] but slightly more relaxed, slightly more open. Above all, do not think of [e] as a closed-up [ɛ].

For a discussion of Italian closed **e**, see [e²] on page 31.

*Exercises 17 and 18*
27

# 19

*Say and sing the following words. Make the
vowels match, but with a slightly wider smile
for the German.*

| English | German | |
|---------|--------|---|
| mitt | mit | [mIt] |
| bit | bitt' | [bIt:t] |
| hissed | bist | [bIst] |
| kissed | ist | [Ist] |
| in | in | [In] |
| bin | bin | [bIn] |

# 20

*Now practice saying and singing the following
German words. Be sure that the vowel* [i]
*finds its proper height.*

| | [i] | | [I] |
|---|-----|---|-----|
| Lied | [lit] | litt | [lIt:t] |
| mied | [mit] | mit | [mIt] |
| ihm | [im] | im | [Im] |
| ihn | [in] | in | [In] |
| stiehlt | [ʃtilt] | stillt | [ʃtIl:lt] |
| bieten | [bi tən] | bitten | [bIt:tən] |
| ihren | [i rən] | irren | [Ir:rən] |

*Tongue vowels*
[I]

[I] Fortunately for American singers, the vowel [I] in German is nearly identical to the English vowel [I] in **mitt**. The German vowel is pronounced with a bit more of a smile.

Note: Remember that for the open [I] Langenscheidt uses [i] (no colon) and for the closed [i] it uses the [i:] (with colon).

The vowel [I] does not exist in French or Italian.

*Exercises 19 and 20*

# 21

*Say and sing the following German words, differentiating among the vowel sounds carefully.*

| | [e] | | [e²] | | [ɛ] |
|---|---|---|---|---|---|
| **wehren** | [ve rən] | **währen** | [ve² rən] | **Wärter** | [vɛr tər] |
| **geben** | [ge bən] | **gäben** | [ge² bən] | **Geld** | [gɛlt] |
| **wer** | [ver] | **wär** | [ve²r] | **Werk** | [vɛrk] |
| **reden** | [re dən] | **Rädern** | [re² dərn] | **retten** | [rɛt:tən] |
| **treten** | [tre tən] | **Tränen** | [tre² nən] | **trennen** | [trɛn:nən] |
| **scheel** | [ʃel] | **Schäfer** | [ʃe² fər] | **Scheffel** | [ʃɛf:fəl] |

# 22

*Practice the following words. The stressed vowels should match.*

| *Italian* | [e²] | *German* | [e²] |
|---|---|---|---|
| **trenta** | [tre²n tɑ] | **Tränen** | [tre² nən] |
| **scemo** | [ʃe² mɔ] | **Schäfer** | [ʃe² fər] |
| **meno** | [me² nɔ] | **Mähne** | [me² nɛ̆] |
| **vero** | [ve² rɔ] | **wäre** | [ve² rɛ̆] |
| **regno** | [re² ɲɔ] | **Räder** | [re² dər] |

[e²]  occurs in German as **ä** closed.

Langenscheidt identifies **ä** closed as [ɛ:], and **ä** open as [ɛ], noting the difference in vowel sounds as a difference in length.  In singing, however, the difference between long and short vowels tends to become somewhat obscured because the length of the vowel is determined by note value and tempo.  In the very same phrase  a short vowel might fall on a long note  and a long vowel on a short note.

In order to differentiate between the long and short forms of **ä**, German singers tend to use [ɛ]  for the short (open), and for the long  they use a vowel which is neither as high as [e] nor as open as [ɛ].  Thus, a distinction is made between **wehren** and **währen**, **geben** and **gäben** on the one hand, and between **Tränen** and **trennen**, **Mähne** and **Männer** on the other.

*Exercise 21*

The only closed **e** sound in Italian is [e²], a relaxed, high **e** which is neither so high as French-German [e] nor so open as [ɛ].  Any doubts about the difference in sound between closed **e** in Italian and closed **e** in German may be dispelled by listening to recordings of Italian opera, sung in Italian by Germans.  Listen especially to the choruses; they have less training in the finer points of pronunciation.  The German [e] is definitely higher.

French has no [e²], only the high [e].  Standard English has [e²] only in combination with other vowels, e.g., the very first vowel sound in **chaotic**.

*Exercise 22*

# 23

*Say the following words, and sing them on equal note values, matching the vowel sounds, from left to right.*

| *English* | *German* | | *French* | | *Italian* | |
|-----------|----------|--|----------|--|-----------|--|
| bell | bellen | [bɛl: lən] | belle | [bɛ lə] | bello | [bɛl:lɔ] |
| bet | Bett | [bɛt: t] | bête | [bɛ tə] | Betto | [bɛt:tɔ] |
| let | letzt | [lɛt: st] | leste | [lɛ stə] | letto | [lɛt:tɔ] |
| pen | Pendel | [pɛn dəl] | peine | [pɛ nə] | penso | [pɛn sɔ] |
| wren | rennen | [rɛn: nən] | reine | [rɛ nə] | rendo | [rɛn dɔ] |
| pear | Perle | [pɛr lĕ] | père | [pɛ rə] | perdo | [pɛr dɔ] |

*Tongue vowels*
[ɛ] [a]


[ɛ]   Here is a vowel sound common to English, Italian, French and German.

*Exercise 23*

When the words in Exercise 23 are spoken (as opposed to sung) from left to right, some vowels may sound a little different from others because of the difference in length (German **bellen** and French **belle**, for example). Other vowels may be affected in speech by a following consonant (English **bell** and German **bellen**). In the sustained diction of singing, consonants should not be allowed to influence the pronunciation of a preceding vowel. Sung **bell** (English) should have the same vowel as **bellen**, **belle** and **bello**. In the same line of thinking, the vowel in French **père** will have a slightly different sound from the vowel in French **belle** in normal speech. That is because **père** has a slightly longer vowel. On a sustained tone, as in singing, the vowels should be identical.

Singers should never spread the vowel [ɛ] so that it sounds like [æ], as in English **cat**. German **Bett** should have a vowel like the [ɛ] in **bet**, not like the [æ] in **bat**.

[a]   The vowel [a] is peculiar to French. German and Italian do not use it at all, nor does standard English. It is a very bright vowel, similar to [ɑ] but pronounced with more of a smile. It may be heard in New England in the pronunciation of words like **ask**, **bath**, **can't**.

# 24

*Try the following words, noting the extra rounding at the end of the American vowel. Maintain this rounding in the corresponding German and French words for a more intense* [u].

| *English* [Uu] | *German* [u] | | *French* [u] | |
|---|---|---|---|---|
| do | du | [du] | doux | [du] |
| two | tu' | [tu] | tout | [tu] |
| rue | Ruh' | [ru] | roux | [ru] |
| moo | muh! | [mu] | moux | [mu] |
| toot | tut | [tut] | toute | [tu tə] |
| moose | Mus | [mus] | mousse | [mu sə] |
| shoe | Schuh | [ʃu] | chou | [ʃu] |
| route | ruht | [rut] | route | [ru tə] |

*Lip vowels*
  [Uu] [u]


Lip vowels   Like [i] the vowel [u] has exactly the same sound in
             French and German, is slightly more relaxed in Italian,
             and is a diphthong in English

     [Uu]    Say English **do**, sustaining the vowel. Watch your lips in a mirror.
             You will see that, at the moment of release of the vowel, the lips
             make a little additional pucker. This extra pucker, which intensifies
             the **oo** sound, is a diphthong glide-off. The American vowel is trans-
             scribed as [Uu].

      [u]    The vowel [u] in French and German takes up where the American
             vowel leaves off. It is very intense and is pronounced with much
             more rounding of the lips and a slightly higher tongue position. **Du**
             in German and **doux** in French should sound to the American ear
             as if they had highly exaggerated vowels. American speech, when it
             is careless, makes very little use of lip projection, and even the best
             English does not utilize the lips to the same extent that German and
             French do.

             The mid-west American [u] tends to be pronounced with the lips
             almost in a smiling position, the jaw high, and with a very marked
             diphthong glide-off. Some natives of Kansas and surrounding states
             almost seem to be pronouncing a German **ü** [y], as in **früh**, or [Y]
             as in **rück**. To avoid such regionalisms, and to approach a good
             English, French, German, or Italian [u], the singer should round his
             lips with a gentle pucker (whistling position), drop the jaw, and feel
             the vowel forward in the mouth, towards the teeth, rather than on
             the hard palate.

      *Exercise 24*

# 25

*Practice the following words, making the* [u]
*more intense as you move from left to right.*

| *English* [Uu] | *Italian* [u] | | *French* [u] | |
|---|---|---|---|---|
| two | tu | [tu] | tout | [tu] |
| poor | pura | [pu ra] | pou | [pu] |
| loon | luna | [lu na] | loup | [lu] |
| boot | butta | [but:ta] | bout | [bu] |
| moor | mura | [mu ra] | moux | [mu] |
| cool | cura | [ku ra] | coup | [ku] |
| doom | dura | [du ra] | doux | [du] |
| goose | gusto | [gu sto] | goût | [gu] |

*Lip vowels*
[u]


[u]   The Italian [u] does not have the exaggerated rounding of the French-German vowel, but it does use more lip rounding than the English vowel. As with all other high and round (closed) vowels, the Italian [u] is more relaxed than its German and French counterparts, but more rounded than its English equivalent. It is, of course, not a diphthong in Italian.

   Note:  Langenscheidt transcribes [u] as [u:] and the open **u** [U] as simply [u] (without colon).

*Exercise 25*

# 26

*Say and sing the following words. Compare the relative openness of the English vowel to the vowels in French and German. There should be no hint of a diphthong in the French and German words. This may be accomplished by avoiding any movement of the lips during the entire length of the vowel sound. In French and German, shape the vowel before you begin to say the word. Use a mirror to watch your lips.*

| *English* [oːu] | *French* [o] | | *German* [o] | |
|---|---|---|---|---|
| grow | gros | [gro] | gross | [groːs] |
| low | l'eau | [lo] | Lohe | [lo ɛ̆] |
| sew | sceau | [so] | so | [zo] |
| bow | beau | [bo] | bot | [bot] |
| boat | beauté | [bo te] | Boot | [bot] |
| loan | l'aune | [lo nə] | Lohn | [lon] |
| dome | dôme | [do mə] | Dom | [dom] |
| phone | faune | [fo nə] | Phonetik | [fo ne tɪk] |

*Lip vowels*
      [o]

[o]    The round vowel [o] exists as the closed **o** in French and German, but does not really exist in standard English. American English substitutes the diphthong [oːu] (as in **row**) for this high, rounded vowel. Elimination of the diphthong glide-off of the English word leaves a vowel which is far too low and unrounded for French and German. The vowel [o] has to be rounded and raised so that it comes closer to the vowel [u] in formation — that is, with an exaggerated pucker. It goes without saying that the French-German [u] must be very high and very rounded, or the [u] and [o] will sound alike.

*Exercise 26*

# 27

Now practice saying and singing the following French and German
words. Do not be afraid to use the lips in what you feel to be an
exaggerated manner. To a native speaker of English, it should feel
exaggerated at first. Form the vowels before you say each word.
Use a mirror. Watch that your lips do not change position for the
duration of each vowel.

First read the words from left to right, contrasting [u] with
[o]. Next read the columns in the order 1,3,2,4, matching vowels
in French and German.

| French | [u] | | [o] | German | [u] | | [o] |
|--------|-----|-----|-----|--------|-----|-----|-----|
| bout | [bu] | beau | [bo] | Buch | [bux] | bot | [bot] |
| moux | [mu] | mot | [mo] | muh! | [mu] | Mohn | [mon] |
| doux | [du] | dos | [do] | du | [du] | Dom | [dom] |
| trou | [tru] | trop | [tro] | trug | [truk] | trog | [trok] |
| route | [ru tə] | rôti | [ro ti] | ruht | [rut] | rot | [rot] |
| fou | [fu] | faut | [fo] | fuhr | [fur] | vor | [for] |
| chou | [ʃu] | chaud | [ʃo] | Schuh | [ʃu] | schon | [ʃon] |
| toute | [tu tə] | tôt | [to] | tut | [tut] | tot | [tot] |
| mousse | [mu sə] | mot | [mo] | Mus | [mus] | Moos | [mos] |

*Lip vowels*
   [o]

[o]   The [o] in French and German should feel the same in singing as
      [u] because the vocal-technical approach should be the same for both
      vowels. Singers who think of [o] as a closed-up [ɔ] will not get
      the vowel high or round enough. Think of [o] as a high and round [u]
      that has been slightly relaxed.

      For a discussion of Italian closed **o**, see [o²].

*Exercise 27*

# 28

[u] *and* [U] *in English*

| [u] | [U] |
|------|------|
| **fool** | **foot** |
| **pool** | **push** |
| **loose** | **look** |
| **boon** | **book** |
| **tooth** | **took** |

# 30

[u] *and* [U] *in German*

| | [u] | | [U] |
|------|------|------|------|
| **Hut** | [hut] | **Hund** | [hUnt] |
| **Kuh** | [ku] | **kund** | [kUnt] |
| **Ruh'** | [ru] | **rund** | [rUnt] |
| **gut** | [gut] | **Gunst** | [gUnst] |
| **Schuh** | [ʃu] | **Schuft** | [ʃUft] |
| **Mus** | [mus] | **muss** | [mUs:s] |
| **Stufe** | [ʃtu fɛ̆] | **Stunde** | [ʃtUn:dɛ̆] |
| **Mut** | [mut] | **Mutter** | [mUt:tər] |

# 29

[U] *in English and German*

| *English* [U] | *German* [U] | |
|------|------|------|
| **bush** | **Busch** | [bUʃ] |
| **look** | **Luchs** | [lUks] |
| **push** | **Husch!** | [hUʃ] |
| **puss** | **muss** | [mUs:s] |
| **put** | **Putz** | [pUt:s] |
| **foot** | **Futter** | [fUt:tər] |

*Lip vowels*
[U]

[U]  The vowel [U] does not occur in Italian or French. It does occur in English and German and is represented by the vowel sound in English **look**. As it occurs so frequently in English, it should be a simple matter to transfer its use into German. The difficulty lies in the fact that this vowel is badly pronounced by many Americans. In every-day speech [U] is pronounced as a quite gutteral vowel with absolutely no lip rounding. In fact, the lips are often pulled back in a smile. The resulting vowel is something between the [ʌ] in **luck** and the [I] in **lick**. The gutteral [U] may be heard loud and clear in the way rock singers pronounce the word **love**. In this remarkable pronunciation **love** and **look** have the same vowel.

The gutteral [U] is not suitable for singing in any language and finds no place in standard English. It does not exist in German.

To find a good [U] for singing, first take the position for [u] with well rounded lips. Now relax the lip rounding slightly, but do not lose it entirely. Keep the tip of the tongue resting against the back of the lower teeth and the back of the tongue arched rather high.

The appropriate sequence for study of this vowel should be:
1. learn to produce a good singable [U] in English by contrasting with English [u].
2. relate this [U] to its use in German words.
3. practice the contrast of [u] and [U] in German words.

Note: Langenscheidt transcribes [U] as [u] (no colon).

*Exercises 28, 29 and 30*

43

# 31

*Use a mirror while practicing saying and singing the following Italian words. Round the lips for each [o²] before you utter the consonant which precedes it. There should be no extra rounding of the lips as you come to the end of the vowel, approaching a consonant. Likewise, the tongue should remain relaxed in the mouth for the entire duration of the vowel.*

| | | | | | |
|---|---|---|---|---|---|
| **voce** | [vo² tʃɛ] | **dono** | [do² nɔ] | **dolore** | [do² lo² rɛ] |
| **nome** | [no² mɛ] | **sotto** | [so²t:tɔ] | **dolorosa** | [do² lo² ro² za] |
| **pompa** | [po²m pa] | **dottore** | [do²t:to² rɛ] | **amore** | [a mo² rɛ] |
| **fonte** | [fo²n tɛ] | **ragione** | [ra dʒo² nɛ] | **amor** | [a mo²r] |
| **ombra** | [o²m bra] | **ragion** | [ra dʒo²n] | **amorosa** | [a mo² ro² za] |

# 32

| English | Italian | | French | | German | |
|---|---|---|---|---|---|---|
| cough | **core** | [kɔ rɛ] | **corps** | [dɔr] | **Korb** | [kɔrp] |
| torpid | **torpido** | [tɔr pi dɔ] | **torpide** | [tɔr pi də] | **Topf** | [tɔpf] |
| jaw | **gioco** | [dʒɔ kɔ] | **joli** | [ʒɔ li] | — | |
| dawn | **donna** | [dɔn:na] | **donne** | [dɔ nə] | **Donner** | [dɔn:nər] |
| corn | **comma** | [kɔm:ma] | **comme** | [kɔ mə] | **komme** | [kɔm:mɛ̆] |
| fall | **folle** | [fɔl:lɛ] | **folle** | [fɔ lə] | **voll** | [fɔl:l] |
| tawny | **tonico** | [tɔ ni kɔ] | **tonique** | [tɔ ni kə] | **Tonne** | [tɔn:nɛ̆] |

*Lip vowels*
[o²] [ɔ]

[o²]   is an arbitrary designation we give to the Italian closed **o**.
Although higher and rounder than open **o** [ɔ], it is not as high
and round as [o] in German and French, but more relaxed.

This vowel exists in English as the first vowel sound in the word
**rowing** quickly pronounced.  Our English diphthong [o:u] tends
to open towards [ɔ:u] when it is sustained.  In an unstressed initial
position, such as in the word **momentum**, we are perhaps closer to a
true [o²].  In Italian, [o²] does not have the diphthong glide-off
that it has in English.  The vowel has the very same sound from beginning to end, and the lips are a little more rounded than in English.

*Exercise 31*

Although [o²] does not exist in standard English, other than in combination with a diphthong glide-off (as in **row** [ro:u]), it may be heard
in the Irish brogue accent in such words as **go**, **so**, etc.  At an Irish or
Scottish breakfast table, [e²] and [o²] may be heard in **bacon** and **toast**.

[ɔ]   As with open **e** [ɛ], open **o** [ɔ] sits astride the four languages.

| English | Italian | French | German |
|---------|---------|--------|--------|
| **port** | **porta** [pɔr tɑ] | **porte** [pɔr tə] | **Pforte** [pfɔr tɛ̆] |

[ɔ] is produced with a dropped jaw  and a rather long vertical mouth
opening.

Americans tend to sing this vowel rather carelessly in all languages
(including English) by allowing the corners of the mouth to widen.
Care should be taken to keep the corners of the mouth drawn in
towards center (fish-mouth) so that the vowel does not begin to
drift in the direction of **ah** and thus lose its identity.

*Exercise 32*

# 33

| *Italian* | *English* | *German* | *French* |
|-----------|-----------|----------|----------|
| fata | father | Vater | fable |
| calma | calm | kam | calin |
| arma | arm | arm | âme |
| banda | barn | Bahn | bas |
| stato | start | Staat | station |

*Lip vowels*
[ɔ] [ɑ]


[ɔ]  English [ɔ] tends to become a diphthong when it occurs before certain consonants (e.g., before the **l** in **fall**). Consequently, in saying these words, English **fall** will not sound exactly like German **voll**, which uses a different kind of [l]. There is also a difference in vowel length. But in singing, the sustained vowel in both words should be identical.

Difference in vowel length will also explain the apparent difference between **dawn**, **donna** and **donne**. In all cases, the sustained singing vowel should be the same.

[ɑ]  is the long, relaxed vowel heard in Italian in words like **sala**, **lana**, **pane**, etc. It is the most relaxed vowel: the jaw is dropped, the lips are totally relaxed, and the tongue lies flat in the mouth with its tip resting against the back of the lower teeth.

*Exercise 33*

# 34

*Practice saying and singing the following
words, making the vowels identical in French
and German. Form the vowels before the consonants. Vowels should have a consistent sound
for their entire duration. If you anticipate the
formation of a following consonant, you will
produce a diphthong.*

| French | | German | |
|---|---|---|---|
| **fût** | [fy] | **für** | [fyr] |
| **tu** | [ty] | **Tür** | [tyr] |
| **mule** | [my lə] | **Mühle** | [my lĕ] |
| **furie** | [fy ri ə] | **führen** | [fy rən] |
| **frugale** | [fry ga lə] | **früh** | [fry] |
| **but** | [by] | **Bühnen** | [by nən] |

# 35

*Say and sing the following pairs of words. Make a very high vowel
on the first word of each pair, then repeat it with a well-rounded
lip position. Then read the columns in the order 1,3,2,4, matching
vowels in French and German.*

| French [i] | | [y] | | German [i] | | [y] | |
|---|---|---|---|---|---|---|---|
| **fit** | [fi] | **fût** | [fy] | **viel** | [fil] | **fühl** | [fyl] |
| **lit** | [li] | **lu** | [ly] | **Lied** | [lit] | **Lüge** | [ly gĕ] |
| **mire** | [mi rə] | **mûre** | [my rə] | **mied** | [mit] | **müde** | [my dĕ] |
| **sire** | [si rə] | **sûre** | [sy rə] | **sieht** | [zit] | **Süd** | [zyt] |
| **salit** | [sa li] | **salut** | [sa ly] | **liegen** | [li gən] | **lügen** | [ly gən] |
| **pire** | [pi rə] | **pure** | [py rə] | **Biene** | [bi nĕ] | **Bühne** | [by nĕ] |

*Mixed vowels*
[y]


[y]   The highest of the mixed vowels [y] occurs in French and German.
Round the lips for [u] and pronounce a very high [i].
The resulting vowel is [y].

Note: Langenscheidt transcribes the closed **ü** [y] as [y:] (with
colon) and the open **ü** [Y] as [y] (without colon).

*Exercises 34 and 35*

# 36

*In the following list, pronounce the words in the first column with a clear, high [e]. Keep the same inner vowel (the same tongue position) and round the lips for [ø], in saying the words in the second column. In going from the first to the second word, do not lock or freeze the tongue into place; rather, let it remain relaxed in place. In going from the second to the third column, the lips should not change. The difference is interior and consists of a lowering and slightly backward repositioning of the tongue.*

|          |        | [e]    |           | [ø]     |           | [o]   |
|----------|--------|--------|-----------|---------|-----------|-------|
| French   | **fée**   | [fe]   | **feu**   | [fø]    | **faut**  | [fo]  |
|          | **j'ai**  | [ʒe]   | **jeu**   | [ʒø]    | **jô**    | [ʒo]  |
|          | **dé**    | [de]   | **deux**  | [dø]    | **dos**   | [do]  |
|          | **né**    | [ne]   | **noeud** | [nø]    | **nos**   | [no]  |
|          | **blé**   | [ble]  | **bleue** | [blø]   | **(ta)bleau** | [blo] |
|          |        |        |           |         |           |       |
| German   | **Ehre**   | [e rɛ̆]  | **Öhren**  | [ø rən]  | **Ohren**  | [o rən]  |
|          | **deren**  | [de rən] | **dösen**  | [dø zən] | **Dosen**  | [do zən] |
|          | **scheel** | [ʃel]    | **schön**  | [ʃøn]    | **schon**  | [ʃon]    |
|          | **kehren** | [ke rən] | **König**  | [kø nIç] | **konisch**| [ko nIʃ] |
|          | **Lehne**  | [le nɛ̆]  | **löhne**  | [lø nɛ̆]  | **Lohn**   | [lon]    |

# 37

*Now try saying and singing the following pairs of words. The vowels should match. If you feel more comfortable in French than in German, read from left to right; if the converse is true, right to left.*

| French   |        | German         |          |
|----------|--------|----------------|----------|
| **jeu**   | [ʒø]   | **schön**        | [ʃøn]    |
| **ceux**  | [sø]   | **Söhnen**       | [zø nən] |
| **veux**  | [vø]   | **(ge)wöhn(lich)** | [vønl]   |
| **queue** | [kø]   | **Köchin**       | [kø çIn] |
| **boeufs**| [bø]   | **Bögen**        | [bø gən] |
| **bleue** | [blø]  | **löhne**        | [lø nɛ̆]  |

*Mixed vowels*
[ø]


[ø]    is exactly the same sound in French and German. Not realizing
        this, singers sometimes say that they have difficulty singing the
        vowel in French **feu** [fø] when they have no apparent difficulty
        with German **schön** [ʃøn]. At times they complain of the
        reverse as well.

        [ø] does not exist in Italian or English.

*Exercises 36 and 37*

## 38

| Form lips for | | sing | English | result | German |
|---|---|---|---|---|---|
| | **rook** | | **Rick** | | **rück** |
| | **brook** | | **brick** | | **Brück**(e) |
| | **took** | | **tick** | | **Tück** |
| | **bush** | | **bish**(op) | | **Büsch**(e) |
| | **look** | | **lick** | | (G)**lück** |

## 39

*Now try the words in the following exercise. First sing the word in the left column, then move the lips forward to the* [U] *position for the word in the second column. Finally, by keeping the same lip position, a slight backing and arching of the back of the tongue will produce the proper vowel for the words in the right column.*

| [I] | | [Y] | | [U] | |
|---|---|---|---|---|---|
| **Kirsch** | [kIrʃ] | **Kürze** | [kYr tsĕ] | **kurz** | [kUrts] |
| **Wirt** | [vIrt] | **Würze** | [vYr tsĕ] | **Wurzel** | [vUr tsəl] |
| **Mitten** | [mIt:tən] | **Mütter** | [mYt:tər] | **Mutter** | [mUt:tər] |
| **misst** | [mIs:st] | **müsst** | [mYs:st] | **musst** | [mUs:st] |
| **Lifte** | [lIf tĕ] | **Lüfte** | [lYf tĕ] | **Luft** | [lUft] |

## 40

*Contrast* [y] *with* [Y] *in the following words:*

| [y] | | [Y] | |
|---|---|---|---|
| **für** | [fyr] | **Fürst** | [fYrst] |
| **Hüte** | [hy tĕ] | **Hütte** | [hYt:tĕ] |
| **fühlen** | [fy lən] | **füllen** | [fYl:lən] |
| **Mühle** | [my lĕ] | **Müller** | [mYl:lər] |
| **kühl** | [kyl] | **küssen** | [kYs:sən] |

*Mixed vowels*
    [Y]




[Y]    Of the four languages under discussion in this book, only German has
       the vowel sound [Y]. It is the open form of the closed vowel [y].
       As such, its formation is very similar to [y], the only difference lying
       in a slightly lower tongue position and a slightly less rounded lip
       position.

           As a mixed vowel, it may be located by combining two other
       vowels which, fortunately, do exist in English. If you assume the
       lip position for [U] and pronounce [I], the resulting vowel will be
       [Y]. Say English **rook**; hold the same lip position and say the name
       **Rick**. The result will be German **rück'**. Care must be taken that the
       lip formation for [U] is that of a good vowel and not that of the
       gutteral [U] discussed earlier.

       *Exercises 38, 39 and 40*

# 41

*Sing the following words. The [ø] words should always have a rounder lip position. The [Y] can be a little more relaxed, but the lips should not lose their roundness entirely.*

| | [ø] | | [Y] |
|---|---|---|---|
| **Höhle** | [hø lĕ] | **Hütte** | [hYt:tĕ] |
| **König** | [kø nIç] | **Künste** | [kYn stĕ] |
| **dösen** | [dø zən] | **düster** | [dYs tər] |
| **Söhne** | [zø nĕ] | **Sünde** | [zYn dĕ] |
| **böse** | [bø zĕ] | **Büsche** | [bY ʃĕ] |
| **Böhme** | [bø mĕ] | **Bünde** | [bYn dĕ] |
| **schön** | [ʃøn] | **Schüssel** | [ʃYs:səl] |
| **Stör** | [ʃtør] | **Stürme** | [ʃtYrmĕ] |

*Mixed vowels*
  [Y] *vs* [ø]




[Y] vs [ø]  Americans often confuse the sound [Y] with the sound [ø].
            Usually  the reason is that [ø] is not round or high enough.
            Indeed Americans often sing [Y] when they think they are singing
            [ø].  In speech the shortness of [Y] and the length of [ø] aid
            in avoiding confusion between the two.  But in singing, both vowels
            could be long, and it is necessary to differentiate between them.

               Note:  Remember Langenscheidt transcribes [Y] (**ü** open) as [y]
            (no colon) and [y] (**ü** closed) as [y:] (with colon).

            *Exercise 41*

# 42

| | | [ɔ] | plus | | [ɛ] | equals | | [œ] |
|---|---|---|---|---|---|---|---|---|
| French | l'or | [lɔr] | | l'air | [lɛr] | | l'heure | [lœr] |
| | mort | [mɔr] | | mer | [mɛr] | | meurt | [mœr] |

| | | | | | | | | |
|---|---|---|---|---|---|---|---|---|
| German | konnte | [kɔn:ntĕ] | | kennte | [kɛn:ntĕ] | | könnte | [kœn:ntĕ] |
| | holla! | [hɔl:la] | | helle | [hɛl:lĕ] | | Hölle | [hœl:lĕ] |
| | stocke | [ʃtɔk:kĕ] | | stecke | [ʃtɛk:kĕ] | | Stöcke | [ʃtœk:kĕ] |

# 43

In the following pairs of French and German
words, the [œ] vowels should match.

| French | | German | |
|---|---|---|---|
| coeur | [kœr] | Körbe | [kœr bĕ] |
| rêveur | [rɛ vœr] | Wörter | [vœr tər] |
| meurt | [mœr] | Mörder | [mœr dər] |
| donneur | [dɔ nœr] | nördlich | [nœrt lIç] |
| seul | [sœl] | Söldner | [zœlt nər] |

# 44

Compare the sound and feel of [ø] and [œ]
in the following pairs:

| German | [ø] | | [œ] |
|---|---|---|---|
| Höhle | [hø lĕ] | Hölle | [hœl:lĕ] |
| Goethe | [gø tĕ] | Götter | [gœt:tər] |
| König | [kø nIç] | können | [kœn:nən] |
| Mörike | [mø rI kĕ] | Mörder | [mœr dər] |
| lösen | [lø zən] | löschen | [lœ ʃən] |

| French | | | |
|---|---|---|---|
| jeu | [ʒø] | jeune | [ʒœ nə] |
| ceux | [sø] | soeur | [sœr] |
| oeufs | [ø] | oeuf | [œf] |
| boeufs | [bø] | boeuf | [bœf] |
| fameux | [fa mø] | meurt | [mœr] |
| deux | [dø] | (ar)deur | [dœr] |

*Mixed vowels*
        [œ]


[œ]   Combining the tongue position of [ɛ] and the lip position of [ɔ]
      will produce [œ]. If you shape your lips for the vowel in English
      **corn** and say the name **Kent**, you will produce German **könnt**.

      The identical vowel exists in French. If you shape the lips for the
      vowel in English **cough** and pronounce English **care**, you will pro-
      duce French **coeur**.

*Exercises 42, 43 and 44*

# 45

*In the following exercises, first say the word in the left-hand column with a well-rounded [ɑ]. Do not pull the corners of the mouth back in a slight smile as you would for [a]. Then, to produce the corresponding word in the right-hand column, merely allow the soft palate to droop, allowing some air to pass through the nasal passages. Jaw, lips, and tongue should not change position between words.*

|        | [ɑ]        |         | [ɑ̃]         |
|--------|-----------|---------|------------|
| **fa**    | [fɑ]      | **fends**  | [fɑ̃]        |
| **la**    | [lɑ]      | **lent**   | [lɑ̃]        |
| **bât**   | [bɑ]      | **banc**   | [bɑ̃]        |
| **sable** | [sɑ blə]  | **semble** | [sɑ̃ blə]    |
| **rafle** | [rɑ flə]  | **renfle** | [rɑ̃ flə]    |
| **lasse** | [lɑ sə]   | **lance**  | [lɑ̃ sə]     |
| **passe** | [pɑ sə]   | **pense**  | [pɑ̃ sə]     |

# 46

*Practice singing the following on very long notes. Be sure that the nasal vowel lasts for the entire duration of the note in each case, and that the following **b** or **p** is executed quickly and clearly.*

| **semble**   | [sɑ̃ blə]     | **jambe**    | [ʒɑ̃ bə]     |
|--------------|-------------|--------------|------------|
| **ambre**    | [ɑ̃ brə]      | **ampleur**  | [ɑ̃ plœr]    |
| **remplace** | [rɑ̃ pla sə] | **remplir**  | [rɑ̃ plir]   |
| **lampe**    | [lɑ̃ pə]      | **campe**    | [kɑ̃ pə]     |

*Nasal vowels*
[ɑ̃]

Nasal vowels   French has four nasalized vowel sounds.
These do not occur in English, Italian or German.

The difference between nasalized and non-nasalized vowels is in the position of the soft palate. Normally, in singing, the soft palate is kept raised so that the stream of air passes entirely through the mouth. For nasalized vowels, however, the soft palate is relaxed so that some air is allowed to pass through the nasal passages as well. The proportion is what determines the amount of nasality of the vowels.

In singing French nasalized sounds, it is a mistake to force air through the nasal passages; this can only result in a peculiar and constricted tone. Good French nasal vowels will be produced when the singer adds some nasality to what is already a well-produced, rounded tone.

[ɑ̃]   It is important to note that the first of the French nasals, [ɑ̃], is based on the Italianate vowel [ɑ], not on the more typically French bright vowel [a].

Note that the **n**'s and **m**'s are silent in the following examples. They are merely spellings to indicate the nasality of the vowels preceding them.

*Exercise 45*

Americans tend to sound the **m** in words like **semble** because they tend to anticipate the formation of the letter **b** after the nasal vowel. **m** and **b** are both labial consonants — that is, they are both formed by touching the lips together. Anticipation of the formation of a **b** (touching the lips together too early) will therefore produce an unwanted **m**. The same is true of **m** followed by **p**.

*Exercise 46*

59

# 47

*Practice singing the following on long notes. Do not anticipate formation of the **d**'s and **t**'s.*

| | | | |
|---|---|---|---|
| **tendre** | [tɑ̃ drə] | **cendre** | [sɑ̃ drə] |
| **demande** | [də mɑ̃ də] | **pendant** | [pɑ̃ dɑ̃] |
| **antique** | [ɑ̃ ti kə] | **antre** | [ɑ̃ trə] |
| **sentier** | [sɑ̃ tje] | **pente** | [pɑ̃ tə] |

# 48

*Practice singing the following words on long notes, avoiding anticipation of [g] and [k].*

| | | | |
|---|---|---|---|
| **encore** | [ɑ̃ kɔ rə] | **ancre** | [ɑ̃ krə] |
| **rencontre** | [rɑ̃ kõ trə] | **anglais** | [ɑ̃ glɛ] |
| **engage** | [ɑ̃ ga ʒə] | **en garde** | [ɑ̃ gar də] |

# 49

*Practice saying and singing the following. The words in the right-hand column should have the same vowel formation as those in the left-hand column. The only difference lies in the added nasality.*

| | | | |
|---|---|---|---|
| **fait** | [fɛ] | **faim** | [fɛ̃] |
| **biais** | [bjɛ] | **bien** | [bjɛ̃] |
| **sait** | [sɛ] | **sein** | [sɛ̃] |
| **mais** | [mɛ] | **main** | [mɛ̃] |
| **fouet** | [fwɛ] | **foin** | [fwɛ̃] |
| **lait** | [lɛ] | **lin** | [lɛ̃] |
| **paix** | [pɛ] | **pain** | [pɛ̃] |

# 50

*Practice singing the following words on long notes. Avoid sounding **m** before **b** or **p**; avoid sounding **n** before **t** or **d**; avoid [ŋ] before [g] or [k].*

| | | | |
|---|---|---|---|
| **timbre** | [tɛ̃ brə] | **impossible** | [ɛ̃ pɔ si blə] |
| **sympathie** | [sɛ̃ pa tiə] | **cymbale** | [sɛ̃ ba lə] |
| **mainte** | [mɛ̃ tə] | **tinte** | [tɛ̃ tə] |
| **pointe** | [pwɛ̃ tə] | **sainte** | [sɛ̃ tə] |
| **teindre** | [tɛ̃ drə] | **peindre** | [pɛ̃ drə] |
| **ingrate** | [ɛ̃ gra tə] | **Poulenc** | [pu lɛ̃k] |

*Nasal vowels*
[ã] [ɛ̃]

Letter **n** (indicating a nasal) occuring before **t** or **d** can also be trouble-some. The formation of [n] , [t] , and [d] is similar. In all three cases the tip of the tongue touches the back of the upper teeth. In a word such as **tendre**, if the **d** is anticipated in its formation, an unwanted **n** will be heard.

*Exercise 47*

If a nasal is followed by the sounds [k] or [g], an unwanted [ŋ] (as in English **sing**) may intrude.

*Exercise 48*

[ɛ̃]   The nasalized vowel [ɛ̃] is based on the sound [ɛ] and has, therefore, the same formation as [ɛ]. Avoid a forced nasality, or the result will be an unpleasant tone.

*Exercises 49 and 50*

# 51

| | | | |
|---|---|---|---|
| **faut** | [fo] | **fond** | [fõ] |
| **pot** | [po] | **pont** | [põ] |
| **mot** | [mo] | **mon** | [mõ] |
| **dos** | [do] | **dont** | [dõ] |
| **beau** | [bo] | **bon** | [bõ] |
| **sceau** | [so] | **son** | [sõ] |
| **allô** | [a lo] | **allons** | [a lõ] |

# 52

*Practice singing the following words on lony notes.*
*Avoid sounding* **m** *before* **b** *and* **p**; *avoid sounding*
**n** *before* **d** *and* **t**; *avoid* [ŋ] *before* [k] *and* [g].

| | | | |
|---|---|---|---|
| **ombre** | [õ brə] | **combien** | [kõ bjɛ̃] |
| **sombre** | [sõ brə] | **nombre** | [nõ brə] |
| **pompe** | [põ pə] | **rompu** | [rõ py] |
| **bonté** | [bõ te] | **conte** | [kõ tə] |
| **monter** | [mõ te] | **fontaine** | [fõ tɛ nə] |
| **conduit** | [kõ dɥi] | **fondu** | [fõ dy] |
| **blonde** | [blõ də] | **profonde** | [prɔ fõ də] |
| **oncle** | [õ klə] | **onction** | [õk sjõ] |
| **ongle** | [õ glə] | **jongleur** | [ʒõ glœr] |

# 53

*Practice the following words on long notes. Pay special attention to*
[œ̃] *followed by* **b**, **p**, **t**, *and* **d**.

| | | | |
|---|---|---|---|
| **un** | [œ̃] | **quelqu'un** | [kɛl kœ̃] |
| **chacun** | [ʃa kœ̃] | **les uns** | [lɛ zœ̃] |
| **un ami** | [œ̃ na mi] | **un doigt** | [œ̃ dwa] |
| **commun** | [kɔ mœ̃] | **parfum** | [par fœ̃] |
| **brun** | [brœ̃] | **défunt** | [de fœ̃] |
| **jeun** | [ʒœ̃] | **emprunt** | [ã prœ̃] |
| **défunte** | [de fœ̃ tə] | **lundi** | [lœ̃ di] |
| **humble** | [œ̃ blə] | **emprunte** | [ã prœ̃ tə] |

*Nasal vowels*
[õ] [œ̃]

[õ]   The formation of the vowel [õ] is the same as that for the non-nasal [o]. The only difference between the two is the added nasality of [õ]. Many persons use a more open nasal [ɔ̃] in French speech. The rounder nasal vowel [õ] is preferable for singing because it avoids a possible confusion with [ɑ̃].

*Exercises 51 and 52*

[œ̃]   The nasal vowel [œ̃] is, of course, the vowel [œ] with nasality added to it. It can be troublesome if the singer has the wrong concept of [œ].

There are two good approaches to finding the correct vowel:

  1. Say [ɔ].
     Keep the same lip formation and say [ɛ].
     The resulting vowel is [œ].
     Now nasalize it to produce [œ̃].

  2. Say [ɔ] as in **law**.
     Keeping the same lip position, say [ɛ̃] as in **lin**.
     The result should be the vowel [œ̃] as in **l'un**.

Americans quite often substitute a grunt which sounds like a nasalized [ʌ]. This incorrect sound uses no projection of the lips and a lower tongue position than [œ]. In careless speech, sometimes the French substitute [ɛ̃] for [œ̃]. Neither of these substitutions is acceptable in correct stage pronunciation.

Fortunately, there are not many words which employ [œ̃], but one of the most common words, the indefinite article **un** does require it.

*Exercise 53*

63

DIPHTHONGS

A diphthong consists of two vowel sounds uttered consecutively within the same syllable. One of these vowels is longer and stronger than the other. Sometimes the stronger comes first, as in the English **boy**; sometimes it is second, as in the English **you**.

In this discussion, we shall use the term *diphthong* to designate the type exemplified by English **boy**, in which the first vowel is the longer and stronger. For the second type, as in **you**, where the second vowel is the longer and stronger, we shall use the term *glide*.

The most important thing to remember about singing diphthongs in any language is that the first vowel of the diphthong should be sustained as long as possible, without any anticipation of the second vowel (the glide-off). Thus, in the English **my** [mɑːi], the [ɑ] is sustained until the last possible moment. Any movement of the tongue, in anticipation of the second vowel, will obscure the principal vowel, make the word more difficult to understand, and interfere with the tone.

Note: remember that the addition of a colon after a phonetic symbol signifies a lengthening of the sound represented by that symbol.

# 54

*Compare:*

| English | Italian | German | French |
|---------|---------|--------|--------|
| [ɑːi] *or* [ɑːI] | [ɑːi] | [ɑːI] *or* [ɑːɛ] | [aj] |
| rye | rai | rein | corail |
| my | mai | Mai | émail |
| find | fai | Feind | travail |
| die | dai | dein | détail |

# 55

| English | Italian | French |
|---------|---------|--------|
| [ɛːi] *or* [ɛːI] | [ɛːi] | [ɛj] |
| say | sei | conseil |
| lay | lei | soleil |
| may | miei | sommeil |
| ray | rei | pareil |
| bay | bei | abeille |

[ɑ:i]    The diphthong [ɑ:i] , as occurring in the English **my**, is also to be used in Italian, as in **mai**. Some singers of English prefer to open the second vowel of the diphthong [ɑ:I]. This opening should not be used in Italian.

[ɑ:I]    There is disagreement among German authorities about the exact identity of the second vowel of this diphthong in German. Siebs identifies it as [ɑ:ɛ]. Langenscheidt uses the more traditional [ɑ:I]. Such hesitation points up the elusive nature of the sound and emphasizes its shortness. Whether [ɑ:ɛ] or [ɑ:I] is used, the second vowel of the diphthong is much lower than the corresponding vowel of the Italian diphthong.

[aj]    The French diphthong does not correspond exactly to the English, Italian or German. The second element of the diphthong has more of a buzz. The tongue is slightly more forward than for the English glide-off.

    Note that in all these languages, there is no difficulty in identifying the first vowel of the diphthong. Differences in opinion occur only over the second vowel because it is so short.

*Exercise 54*

[ɛ:i]    The diphthong [ɛ:i], occurring in English **day**, may also be used in Italian **dei**. Singers who prefer to open the second vowel of the diphthong in English [dɛ:I] should not do so in Italian.

[ɛj]    The French diphthong [ɛj] is quite similar but ends with a buzz. This diphthong does not occur in German.

*Exercise 55*

# 56

*Practice saying and singing:*

deuil    seuil    fauteuil    orgueil    oeil    oeillet

# 57

*Practice saying and singing:*

fenouil    souille    bouillon

# 58

*Practice:* [ɔ] — [i]  [ɔ] — [u]  [ɔ] — [y]

| *English* | *Italian* | *German* |
|---|---|---|
| [ɔ:i] *or* [ɔ:I] | [ɔ:i] | [ɔ:y] *or* [ɔ:ø] |
| annoy | noi | neu |
| point | poi | — |
| envoy | voi | — |
| boy | — | beute |
| Troy | — | treu |
| alloy | — | läuten |
| Roy | — | Reu' |
| coy | — | keusch |
| ahoy | — | heute |

[œj]    The diphthong [œj] does not occur in English, Italian or German. As with other French diphthongs, the second element is a palatal buzz, with the tongue arched well forward in the mouth.

*Exercise 56*

[uj]    The diphthong [uj] occurs only in French.

*Exercise 57*

[ɔ:i]    The diphthong [ɔ:i], occurring in English **boy** is also used in Italian
[ɔ:I]    **poi**. Singers who prefer to open the second vowel in English ([bɔ:I] rather than [bɔ:i]) should not make this opening in Italian.

[ɔy]    German authorities differ about this diphthong. Langenscheidt uses [ɔy], Siebs recommends [ɔø]. The latter can be very difficult for Americans to execute, and [ɔy] serves very well for singing. The important thing to remember is that the second element of the diphthong is rounder than the corresponding sound in English.

[ɔ:y]    To arrive at [ɔ:y], begin the first vowel with a good [ɔ] formation. The lips project, the corners of the mouth are drawn in towards center, and the jaw is dropped. Now move towards [i], but as you do so, direct the lips towards a pucker. As the jaw rises for [i], the lips round for [u].

    This diphthong does not exist in French.

*Exercise 58*

**59**

| English | Italian | German |
|---|---|---|
| [ɑ:u] *or* [ɑ:ʊ] | [ɑ:u] | [ɑ:ʊ] *or* [ɑ:o] |
| ow! | aura | auch |
| bow | bau | bauen |
| found | fausto | Faust |
| cow | causa | Kauf |
| loud | Laura | laut |

*Diphthongs*
[ɑ:u] [ɑ:U]

[ɑ:u]   The diphthong [ɑ:u], occurring in English **cow**, is also used in Italian
         **aura**.  Singers who prefer to open the second vowel of the diphthong
[ɑ:U]   in English ([ɑ:U] rather than [ɑ:u])  should not make this opening
         in Italian.

    Siebs identifies this diphthong in German as [ɑo].  Langenscheidt
uses the more traditional [ɑU].  The use of [ɑ:o] can be very helpful
in executing high notes.

    This diphthong does not exist in French.

*Exercise 59*

# 60

Compare the following English and German words. The initial sound in each of the German words should have more buzz than in the English.

| English | German | |
|---------|--------|---|
| yacht | ja | [jɑ] |
| young | jung | [jʊŋ] |
| yoke | Joch | [jɔx] |
| you | Jude | [ju dĕ] |
| yowl | jauchzen | [jɑːʊx tsən] |
| Danube | Jubel | [ju bəl] |

# 61

Compare the following Italian and French words. In each case, the French [j] should have more buzz.

| Italian | | French | |
|---------|---|--------|---|
| fiero | [fjɛ rɔ] | fier | [fjɛr] |
| ieri | [jɛ ri] | hier | [jɛr] |
| miele | [mjɛ lɛ] | miel | [mjɛl] |
| fiacco | [fjɑkːɔ] | fiacre | [fja krə] |
| niente | [njɛn tɛ] | canadienne | [ka na djɛ nə] |
| tiene | [tjɛ nɛ] | tienne | [tjɛ nə] |
| aiuto | [ɑ ju tɔ] | payer | [pɛ je] |

GLIDES

A short vowel followed immediately by a long, strong vowel
in the same syllable is called a glide. Sometimes glides are referred to
as semi-consonants or semi-vowels. Glides are really simple vowel
sounds which become intensified as they rush towards a following
vowel.

[j]   is a glide that occurs in English, Italian, French and German.
It is an intensified [i]. If you prolong the first letter in English **yes**,
you will find yourself pronouncing [i].

This glide does not sound exactly the same in all four languages.
In French and German the sound is produced with the tongue arched
forward in the mouth so that a palatalized buzzing is produced. In
English and Italian the arching of the tongue takes place farther back
so that there is no buzz.

*Exercises 60 and 61*

# 62

*Use a more extended lip formation for an intense [w] in the French words.*

| English | Italian | | French | |
|---------|---------|---|--------|---|
| we | **qui** | [kwi] | **oui** | [wi] |
| west | **questo** | [kwɛ stɔ] | **ouest** | [wɛst] |
| twenty | **tuona** | [twɔ na] | **toi** | [twa] |
| quell | **quello** | [kwɛl:lɔ] | **coiffe** | [kwa fə] |
| swell | **suolo** | [swɔ lɔ] | **soit** | [swa] |
| — | **nuoce** | [nwɔ tʃɛ] | **noir** | [nwar] |

# 63

*To practice a word like* **nuit***, pretend that it has two syllables:* **nu — it***. Sing the word, holding the first vowel long enough to establish a good [y]. Now repeat the word over and over, shortening the first vowel a little more each time until you have it gliding into the second.*

*Try the same exercise on the following words:*

| | | | | |
|---|---|---|---|---|
| **lui** | **suis** | **puis** | **cuit** | **fuit** |
| **huit** | **luit** | **buis** | **bruit** | **truite** |
| **puisque** | **nuage** | **muet** | **sueur** | **tué** |

# 64

*Italian words using this glide are:*

| | | | | | |
|---|---|---|---|---|---|
| **gli** | [ʎi] | **aglio** | [a ʎo] | **consiglio** | [kon si ʎo] |
| **foglio** | [fɔ ʎo] | **soglia** | [sɔ ʎa] | **migliore** | [mi ʎo rɛ] |

*Glides*
[w] [ɥ] [ʎ]

[w] The [w] glide occurs in English, Italian and French, but not in German. The sound is approximately the same in all three languages, except for a subtle difference: in French the [w] is pronounced with slightly more extended lips so that the sound is more intense. [w] is an intensified [u]. If you prolong the first letter in English **we**, you will find yourself pronouncing [u].

*Exercise 62*

[ɥ] This glide occurs only in French, as an intensified [y] when **u** is followed by another vowel, as in **nuit**. Americans often have trouble with it, and a common error for American singers is to substitute [w] for [ɥ].

   The way out of the error is to remember that [ɥ] is nothing more than an intensified [y], in the same way that [w] is an intensified [u], and [j] is an intensified [i].

*Exercise 63*

[ʎ] This sound exists in Italian, but not in French or German. It does not commonly exist in American speech. [ʎ] is a compressed version of two sounds: [l] and [j]. We encounter them in succession in English between words, as in the sequence **all you** or **real union**. In Italian, the two sounds are uttered almost simultaneously, with a light [l] uttered in the same syllable as the following light [j].

   This sound does not often occur in the English spoken in the United States. A careful speaker (or singer) will use it in words like **allure**, **lute**, **lewd**, etc. The British use it in **aluminium** but Americans do not in **aluminum**.

*Exercise 64*

# 65

*Practice the following words, prolonging the vowel preceding* [ɲ] *as long as possible. Execute the* [ɲ] *quickly and with energetic intensity.*

| *Italian* | | *French* | |
|---|---|---|---|
| **segno** | [se ɲɔ] | **saigne** | [sɛ ɲə] |
| **bagno** | [bɑ ɲɔ] | **bagne** | [bɑ ɲə] |
| **regno** | [re ɲɔ] | **régner** | [re ɲe] |
| **pegno** | [pe ɲɔ] | **peigne** | [pɛ ɲə] |
| **cognito** | [kɔ ɲi tɔ] | **cogne** | [kɔ ɲə] |
| **vigna** | [vi ɲɑ] | **vigne** | [vi ɲə] |

*Glides*
[ɲ]

[ɲ]  As with the preceding glide, [ɲ] is a combination of two sounds, tight-
ly compressed and uttered almost simultaneously. The sounds are
[n] and [j]. In English we encounter this succession of sounds in a
few words, but we tend to pronounce it lazily, without the intensity
or the speed it possesses in Italian and French.

For English **onion**, we pronounce [ʌn jən]. For **ognuno**, an
Italian pronounces [o ɲu no], for **oignon**, a Frenchman pronounces [ɔ ɲõ].

A careful speaker (or singer) of English will pronounce **new** [ɲu],
**nuisance** [ɲu səns], **numerous** [ɲu mə rəs]. Usually, however, we
do not hear the sound [ɲ] in American speech.

*Exercise 65*

77

# TABLE OF VOICED AND UNVOICED CONSONANTS

| *voiced* | *unvoiced* |
|----------|------------|
| [b] | [p] |
| [d] | [t] |
| [g] | [k] |
| [v] | [f] |
| [ʒ] | [ʃ] |
| [z] | [s] |
| [j] | [ç] |
| [R] | [x] |
| — | [h] |
| [m] | — |
| [n] | — |
| [ŋ] | — |
| [l] | — |
| [r] | — |
| [dʒ] | [tʃ] |
| [dz] | [ts] |

# CONSONANT CLASSIFICATION

Singers, especially Americans, need always to be reminded that consonants must be articulated with more energy in singing than in speech. The larger the auditorium, the more the intensity needed. Singing with orchestra demands more than singing with a piano. On the other hand, over-articulation of consonants in a small room will sound exaggerated and unnatural, and is to be guarded against. Usually, however, singers err in the other direction.

The production of clearly articulated consonants need not result in a merciless chopping of the vocal line. A mere lengthening of the consonant sounds (which steals precious time from the vowels) does not, in many cases, improve the consonants. In fact, with some consonants, (particularly the plosives), an unnecessary lengthening will even obscure the articulation. The goal should be execution in a manner clear, clean and crisp—one which takes as little time as possible.

Consonants may be voiced or unvoiced. When the vocal chords are in vibration during the articulation of a consonant, we call it voiced. It has a pitch. Normally, it should have the same pitch as the vowel which follows it.

A consonant which is articulated without attendant vibration of the vocal chords is unvoiced. It has no pitch.

# 66

*Practice the following words. Hold a finger in front of your mouth. You should feel the puff of air after each* [p].

| English | German | |
|---------|--------|--------|
| pow! | pauken | [pɑːU kən] |
| pelt | Pelz | [pɛlts] |
| peep | piepen | [pi pən] |
| poke | pochen | [pɔ xən] |
| puts | Putz | [pUt:s] |

# 67

*Now practice the following words. Hold a finger in front of your mouth. You should feel no puff of air after the* [p].

| Italian | | French | |
|---------|--------|--------|--------|
| papa | [pɑ pɑ] | pas | [pɑ] |
| periglio | [pe ri ʎɔ] | péril | [pe ril] |
| possibile | [pos:si bi lɛ] | possible | [pɔ si blə] |
| pulce | [pul tʃɛ] | pousse | [pu sə] |

# FORMING AND COMPARING CONSONANTS

*Plosives*   A plosive is a sound articulated by:
         1. forming the consonants with the lips, tongue, teeth
         2. compressing air behind lips or tongue, and
         3. exploding the air
In everyday American speech we often implode many consonants; that is, we execute steps 1 and 2, but do not execute step 3. Implosion is to be avoided by anyone wishing clear diction in singing.

[b] [p]   These two consonant sounds are formed by touching the lips together, compressing air behind them, and exploding it. The soft palate should be raised and the cheeks relaxed.

If the soft palate is allowed to droop during the articulation of these consonants, there is a danger of sounding an unwanted [m] before the [b] or [p], since [m] is also produced by touching the lips together. Be especially careful of the voiced [b]. Absolutely no air may pass through the nasal passages or **robe** [ro:ub] becomes [ro:umb].

The treatment of these consonants in Germanic languages (English and German) differs slightly from their treatment in Romance languages (Italian and French). In English we insert a little puff of air between the consonant and a following vowel. The same is true of German. In Italian and French there is no puff of air, and the exploded consonant is followed immediately by the vowel. This dryness is more obvious with [p] than with [b].

*Exercises 66 and 67*
*81*

# 68

*French:* **pire** [pi rə]    **pure** [py rə]
         **pièce** [pjɛ sə]    **puis** [pyi]

*Contrast these with Italian, where the consonants remain explosively dry.*

*Italian:* **pira** [pi rɑ]    **pura** [pu rɑ]
          **pietà** [pje tɑ]

# 69

*Compare the sound of* [d] *and* [t] *in the following words. Use alveolar consonants for the English and German; dental consonants for the Italian and French.*

| English | German | | Italian | | French | |
|---------|--------|---|---------|---|--------|---|
| two | tu' | [tu] | tu | [tu] | tout | [tu] |
| do | du | [du] | dura | [du rɑ] | doux | [du] |
| talent | Tal | [tɑl] | tale | [tɑ lɛ] | talon | [ta lõ] |
| desk | des | [dɛs] | desto | [dɛs tɔ] | destin | [dɛs tɛ̃] |
| tote | tot | [tot] | totale | [to tɑlɛ] | tôt | [to] |

# 70

*Compare the sound of:*

*Italian (dental and dry)*      *French (dental and buzzy)*

| **ti** | [ti] | **tire** | [ti rə] |
|--------|------|----------|---------|
| **intimo** | [in ti mɔ] | **intime** | [ɛ̃ ti mə] |
| **tiene** | [tjɛ nɛ] | **tiens** | [tjɛ̃] |
| **tu** | [tu] | **tu** | [ty] |
| **turco** | [tur kɔ] | **turc** | [tyrk] |
| **tue** | [tu:ɛ] | **tué** | [tɥe] |

*Plosives*
[d] [t]

In French, because of the extreme height of the vowels [i] and [y], and the glides [j] and [ɥ], we do hear an intrusion of air *within* the consonant sounds.

### Exercise 68

[d] [t]   As before, this pair of consonants is formed one way in Germanic languages and another in Romance languages.

*English and German:* the tip of the tongue is placed against the hard gum ridge directly in back of the upper teeth. Air is compressed behind the tongue and then released sharply. [t] and [d] formed in this manner are called alveolar [t] and [d]. It is unnecessary and wasteful to expel air from the lungs in articulating [t] and [d]; merely use the air in the mouth itself.

*Italian and French:* the [d] and [t] are dental. That is, the tip of the tongue is flattened against the back of the upper teeth. This produces a sound which is dryer than the English-German sound.

### Exercise 69

In French the extreme height of [i] and [y] and their glides [j] and [ɥ] encourages a palatalization of [d] and [t] when they occur before these vowels. The [d] and [t] are still formed on the teeth, but they do not sound as dry as they do before other vowels. There is now more air within the consonant sound. These palatalized **d**'s and **t**'s should not, of course, sound like [ts] or [dz].

### Exercise 70

83

# 71

*Compare the following words:*

| English | Italian | | French | |
|---------|---------|------|--------|------|
| cop | capo | [ka pɔ] | cap | [kap] |
| kelp | che | [kɛ] | quel | [kɛl] |
| corn | corno | [kɔr nɔ] | corne | [kɔr nə] |
| coop | cupo | [ku pɔ] | coupe | [ku pə] |

# 72

*Compare:*

| Italian (dry) | | French (airy) | |
|---------------|------|---------------|------|
| chi | [ki] | qui | [ki] |
| ghigna | [gi ɲa] | Guy | [gi] |
| chiave | [kja ˌvɛ] | quiet | [kjɛ] |
| cura | [ku ra] | cure | [ky rə] |
| cui | [ku:i] | cuit | [kɥi] |

*Plosives*
[g] [k]

[g] [k]    These two consonants are formed the same way in all four languages. As with the other plosives, there is a puff of air between the consonant and a vowel which follows it in English and German. In Italian and French  the sound is dryer; there is no puff of air. Again, the lack is more obvious with the unvoiced consonant [k] than with the voiced [g].

*Exercises 71 and 72*

Summary of the plosives    English and German    a puff of air between consonant and vowel.  [d] and [t] are formed on the gum ridge (alveolar).

Italian    always dry; no puff of air.  [d] and [t] are dental.

French    dry except before [i], [j], [y], [ɥ]. [d] and [t] are dental.

# 73

*Practice with the following words.*

| English | Italian | | French | | German | |
|---------|---------|---|--------|---|--------|---|
| fury | fumo | [fu mɔ] | fumer | [fy me] | fünf | [fʏnf] |
| final | finale | [fi nɑ lɛ] | final | [fi nal] | finster | [fɪn stər] |
| fanfare | affetto | [ɑf:fɛt:tɔ] | fanfare | [fã fa rə] | offen | [ɔf:fən] |
| vine | vino | [vi nɔ] | vin | [vɛ̃] | Winter | [vɪn tər] |
| vase | vaso | [vɑ zɔ] | vase | [vɑ zə] | wachsen | [vɑk sən] |
| valve | avvenire | [ɑv:ve ni rɛ] | vivant | [vi vã] | Waffen | [vɑf:fən] |

# 74

*Contrast the consonants in the following words.  Round the lips to make the [ ʃ ] and [ ʒ ] darker in French and German.*

| English | Italian | | French | | German | |
|---------|---------|---|--------|---|--------|---|
| shoe | sciupo | [ʃu pɔ] | chou | [ʃu] | Schuh | [ʃu] |
| shah | scialo | [ʃɑ lɔ] | chat | [ʃa] | Schar | [ʃɑr] |
| shirt | scendo | [ʃɛn dɔ] | fâcheuse | [fɑ ʃø zə] | schön | [ʃøn] |
| measure | — | | juger | [ʒy ʒe] | — | |
| asia | — | | agir | [a ʒir] | — | |
| pleasure | — | | piège | [pjɛ ʒə] | — | |

*Fricatives*
[v] [f] [ʒ] [ʃ]

Fricatives   A fricative is a consonant caused by the friction of air against teeth, tongue or palate.

[v] [f]   are formed the same way in all four languages.
In trying to intensify these sounds singers often make the mistake of clamping down on the lower lip with the upper teeth. This interferes with the passage of air and reduces the friction which causes the sound. It also creates unnecessary tensions.

A good way to form [v] and [f] is to place the upper teeth behind the lower lip. The lips can then be relaxed as air is blown past them.

*Exercise 73*

[ʒ] [ʃ]   There is a subtle difference between these consonants in English and Italian on the one hand, and in French and German on the other.

In French and German the lips are more puckered (more protruding), and the tongue is pulled back away from the lower teeth. The resulting sound is darker and richer than we are accustomed to in English and Italian.

[ʒ] does not exist in Italian and German, except in borrowed words.

*Exercise 74*

# 75

*Practice the following German words, making a clear distinction between [ç] and [ʃ].*

| | [ç] | | [ʃ] | | [ʃ] [ç] |
|---|---|---|---|---|---|
| **wich** | [vIç] | **Wisch** | [vIʃ] | **schüchtern** | [ʃYç tərn] |
| **mich** | [mIç] | **misch** | [mIʃ] | **sprich** | [ʃprIç] |
| **dich** | [dIç] | **Tisch** | [tIʃ] | **sprichst** | [ʃprIçst] |
| **keuche** | [kɔ:y çɛ] | **keusche** | [kɔ:y ʃɛ] | **Storch** | [ʃtɔrç] |
| | | | | **Stich** | [ʃtIç] |
| | | | | **sprechen** | [ʃprɛ çən] |
| | | | | **schrecklich** | [ʃrɛk:klIç] |

*Fricatives*
[z] [s] [ç]

[z] [s]     In spoken German the [z] and [s] are dental, i.e., articulated with the tip of the tongue on the back of the upper teeth. This is not a desirable production for singing. It creates consonants with too much hiss and can also result in a lisp. In singing German, therefore, these consonants are produced as in singing Italian, French and English.

[ç]     The consonant [ç] does not exist in Italian or French. We approach it in English if we pronounce words like **human**, **Hubert**, **hue** with a greatly exaggerated **h**.

    The tongue is arched well forward in the mouth; the tip of the tongue is against the back of the lower teeth; the lips are in a smiling position. The sound is caused by the friction of air passing between the arched tongue and the hard gum ridge directly in back of the upper teeth.

    [ç] occurs in German words like **ich** [Iç], **reich** [rɑːIç], **Knecht** [knɛçt], **Milch** [mIlç], **leuchten** [lɔːIç tən], **Nächte** [nɛç tɛ̃].

[ç] [ʃ]     [ç] should never be confused with [ʃ]. The two sounds are really quite different from each other. [ç] has the tongue forward, while [ʃ] has the tongue retracted. For [ç] the lips are pulled back in a smile; for [ʃ] the lips are rounded. For [ç] direct the stream of air against the gum ridge and upper teeth; for [ʃ] direct the stream of air against the lower teeth.

    If [ç] is voiced (if it receives a pitch), it becomes [j].

For a discussion of [j], see page 73.

*Exercise 75*

89

# 76

*Practice* [x] *in the following German words:*

| | | | |
|---|---|---|---|
| ach | noch | Buch | auch |
| Nacht | doch | Tuch | Rauch |
| lachen | pochen | suchen | tauchen |
| lache | poche | suche | Hauch |

*Contrast* [ç] *with* [x] *in the following words:*

| [ç] | [x] |
|---|---|
| mich | mach' |
| dich | doch |
| recht | raucht |
| Wicht | wacht |
| sich | such' |
| Nächte | Nacht |
| wächte | wacht |
| Gesträuche | Strauch |

*Fricatives*
[R] [x] [h]

[R]    is a sound which is not used in singing. It is the uvular **r** heard
in Parisian speech. Sometimes an ill-informed singer (not French)
will try to use this [R] in singing "to make the style very French".
It is used only by cabaret and music-hall singers and has no place
in the style of diction used in opera or in song literature. Its use
in these forms is considered quite vulgar.

     Likewise, [R] is not used in singing German, although it may be
heard in German speech.

     In singing French or German use a flipped or trilled [r], depending
on circumstances, just as in Italian.

[x]    is an unvoiced and very short [R]. It does not exist in English,
French or Italian. It is the final sound in the Scottish word **loch**. It
is somewhat similar to [h], but with the extreme back of the tongue
raised so that, in passing through the throat, the expelled air makes
more of a sound. It need not be so violent as the sound of preparing
to spit.

[h]    is formed like [x], but with the back of the tongue depressed.
It is the sound familiar to us in English words like **home**, **house**, etc.

*Exercise 76*

*Nasals*
[m] [n]


Nasals A nasal consonant is one in which the air stream is directed
through the nasal passages rather than through the mouth.

[m]   is the same sound in English, Italian, French and German, and
it should be produced the same way.  [m] is a humming sound produced by expelling air through the nasal passages  while the vocal chords
are vibrating and the lips are lightly touched together.  Some singers
press their lips together.  This accomplishes nothing for diction and
only causes unnecessary tension.  There is no need to clamp the lips
together, merely touch them.

If [m] is not clear, either
1. it is not sounding long enough, or
2. the pitch is not clear.

[n]   In English, [n] is usually formed by placing the tip of the tongue
against the hard gum ridge directly in back of the upper teeth, expelling air through the nasal passages, and vibrating the vocal chords. In
Italian, French  and German, the [n] is dental; that is, the tip of the
tongue is placed against the back of the upper teeth.  The difference
in sound is subtle, but the dental [n] will be more resonant.

As with [m], the amount of pressure exerted has nothing to do
with the audibility of the consonant.  If [n] is not clear, as with [m],
it must either be lengthened or pitched more distinctly.

# 77

*Compare the use of* [ŋ] *in the following words:*

| *English* | *Italian* | |
|---|---|---|
| rank | anche | [aŋ kɛ] |
| anchor | ancora | [aŋ ko ra] |
| monk | monco | [moŋ kɔ] |
| dunk | dunque | [duŋ kwɛ] |
| finger | fingo | [fiŋ gɔ] |
| tango | angoscia | [aŋ go ʃa] |
| fang goes | fango | [faŋ gɔ] |
| *(not* fan goes*)* | | |
| lung goes | lungo | [luŋ gɔ] |

| *English* | *German* | |
|---|---|---|
| thank you | danke | [daŋ kɛ̆] |
| thinking | denken | [dɛŋ kən] |
| fink | Fink | [fIŋk] |
| punctual | Punkt | [pUŋkt] |

*Nasals*
[ŋ]

[ŋ]   is the sound found at the end of English **ring**. There is no [g]
      explosion after it. Besides English, the sound also occurs in Italian
      and German. It does not exist in French.

      In English we use the sound [ŋ] for the spelling **ng**. We also use
      it when **n** occurs before [k] or [g]. For instance, we pronounce
      **thank** as if it were spelled **thangk**. We pronounce **finger** as if it were
      spelled **fing-ger**. (Note that there is no [g] in **singer**.)

      The same thing happens in Italian and German. Italian **anche**
      [aŋkɛ] is pronounced as if it were spelled **angche**. German **danke**
      [daŋkɛ̃] is pronounced as if it were spelled **dangke**.

*Exercise 77*

# 78

*Compare the* [l] *sounds in the following words. Keep them bright in German.*

| English | German | |
|---|---|---|
| all | alle | [ɑl:lɛ] |
| old | alte | [ɑl tɛ] |
| temple | Tempel | [tɛm pəl] |
| halt | halt | [hɑlt] |
| hold | holde | [hɔl dɛ̆] |
| helm | Helm | [hɛlm] |
| mild | mild | [mɪlt] |

| English | Italian | | French | |
|---|---|---|---|---|
| alto | alto | [ɑl ɔ] | altérer | [al te re] |
| colt | coltello | [kol tɛl:lɔ] | col | [kɔl] |
| filter | filtro | [fil trɔ] | filtre | [fil trə] |
| cultivate | coltivando | [kol ti vɑn dɔ] | cultiver | [kyl ti ve] |
| ultimate | ultimo | [ul ti mɔ] | ultime | [yl ti mə] |

[l]   In English there are at least two sounds for the letter **l**.
When it occurs before a vowel, we usually pronounce it with the
tongue quite relaxed, the tip of the tongue against the hard gum
ridge, the sides of the tongue turned down slightly to allow air to
pass laterally. To test this, notice the position of the tongue as you
are about to say **liquid**.

Now say **all**, and you will see that for a final **l** (and also for **l** before
a consonant, as in **milk**), the tongue has quite a different position, and
the **l** has a much darker sound. The tip of the tongue is still against
the gum ridge, but now there is a deep depression down the center
of the tongue, which is arched toward the back of the mouth.
The root of the tongue is depressed.

This dark **l** should not be used in Italian, French or German.
Americans often use it unconsciously when **l** is final or before
a consonant.

In Italian, French and German the [l] is dental—that is, the tip of
the tongue rests on the back of the upper teeth. It is completely
relaxed and quite high and forward in the mouth. There is no
depression nor arching. The same liquid, forward sound is used for [l]
in all positions, final as well as before consonants.

Note: In Italian and French, [d], [n], [t] and [l] are DeNTaL
consonants. In German only [n] and [l] are dental.

*Exercise 78*

# 79

*A good way to approach the problem of rolling is to start from familiar English words beginning with* **thr**. *Pronounce* **three** *slowly as if it were spelled* **thdee**, *substituting* **d** *for* **r**. *You will find that the tongue moves back away from the upper teeth to the hard gum ridge for the* **d**. *Now repeat this several times, each time using a lighter* **d**. *Do not stop between the* **th** *and the* **d**. *Eventually, if you keep your tongue relaxed, you will arrive at a perfectly acceptable flipped* **r**.

   *The next step is to try the same procedure with other similar English words such as* **through, thrill, thrust, throw, thread,** *etc. When you feel comfortable with the flipped* **r** *in these words, try omitting the* **th***:* **rust, row, red,** *etc. Then on to Italian words, always keeping the flipped* **r***:* **ara, cara, rara, mare, care, cure, mura, dura, dure, duri, duro,** *etc.*

# 80

*Practice the following with a double flip:*

| arte | sorte | morto | dormi | urna |
| corno | torno | arpa | stirpe | ardo |

*and French:*

| dormir | parlez | armez | fermez | tournez |
| turban | clarté | fierté | merlin | sortez |

*and German:*

| arme | ferne | gerne | Perle | Herz |
| Schmerz | erst | hörte | durch | Wurst |

[r]   is the symbol for the flipped **r**. American **r** is never used in Italian, French or German.

    Sometimes Americans have difficulty in learning to flip or roll an **r**. There have been several ways suggested, such as trying to imitate a doorbell or a motorboat.

Italian words which have **r** occurring before a consonant will need a double flip. This takes more breath pressure.

A fully rolled **r** (trilled **r**) is simply a matter of adding more breath pressure. At first you will use too much breath, but after you get the rolled **r** started, you will learn how to control the amount of breath used, so that there is no waste.

*Exercises 79 and 80*

# 81

| Italian | | German | |
|---|---|---|---|
| **zio** | [tsi:ɔ] | **ziehen** | [tsi ən] |
| **zucchero** | [tsuk:kɛrɔ] | **Zucker** | [tsUk:kər] |
| **zitti** | [tsit:ti] | **zieht** | [tsit] |
| **razza** | [rɑt:sɑ] | **kratzen** | [krat:sən] |

Affricates　　An affricate is a combination of a plosive and a fricative.

[dʒ]　　is the initial sound in English **gem** and **jury**. The same sound
　　　　occurs in Italian in words like **gemo** and **giusto**. It does not exist in
　　　　French or German.

[tʃ]　　is the unvoiced counterpart occurring in English, spelled as **ch** in
　　　　words like **choose** and **church**. The same sound occurs in Italian in
　　　　words like **cena** and **ciampa**. It does not exist in French.

　　　　In German [tʃ] occurs only rarely and is spelled **tsch**. [tʃ] is
　　　　found in words like **deutsch** [dɔ:ytʃ], **plätschert** [plɛ tʃərt] and
　　　　**zwitschert** [tsvɪ tʃərt].

[dz]　　occurs in English as the last sound in **heads** and **beds**. In
　　　　Italian the same sound occurs in some words spelled with a **z**:
　　　　**zelo** [dze lɔ], **zeffiretti** [dzef:fi ret:ti], **mezzo** [mɛd:zɔ] and
　　　　**azzurro** [ɑd:zur:rɔ].
　　　　This sound does not exist in French or German.

[ts]　　occurs as the final sound in English **eats** and occurs twice in
　　　　**tsetse fly**. In Italian and German the sound is spelled **z**.

*Exercise 81*

# 2 Applying the sounds

# Italian

This section, based on grammatical and linguistic sources and on the common usage of the best singers of our time, is intended as a guide to the singing pronunciation of Italian. Some of the rules do not apply to the spoken language.

*(Exercise numbers are in bold face)*

| | | | | | | | |
|---|---|---|---|---|---|---|---|
| **a** | 115 **33** | **gg** | 138-139 | | | **qu** | 132 149 **62** |
| **ae** | 129 | **gh** | 140 **72** | | | **r** | 148 **79 80** |
| **ai** | 129 **54** | **gi** | 131 141 | | | **rr** | 138-139 148 **79** |
| **ao** | 129 | **gli** | 131-132 **64** | | | | |
| **au** | 129 **59** | **gn** | 149 **65** | | | **s** | 143-144 |
| | | | | | | **sc** | 140 |
| | | **h** | 146 | | | **sce** | 141 **74** |
| **b** | 138 142 | | | | | **sci** | 141 **74** |
| **bb** | 138 142 | **i** | 115 131-133 **15 61** | | | **si** | 144 |
| | | | | | | **ss** | 138-139 |
| **c** | 138 140-141 **71 72** | **j** | 131 146 | | | **st** | 142 |
| **cc** | 138-139 | | | | | | |
| **ce** | 141 | **l** | 146 **78** | | | **t** | 138 142 **69 70** |
| **ch** | 140 **72** | **ll** | 138-139 | | | **tt** | 138-139 |
| **ci** | 131 141 | | | | | | |
| | | **m** | 147 | | | **u** | 115 131-133 **25 62** |
| **d** | 138 142 **69** | **mm** | 138-139 147 | | | | |
| **dd** | 138-139 | | | | | **v** | 149 **73** |
| | | **n** | 147 | | | **vv** | 138-139 |
| **e** | 116-120 126-128 **22 23** | **nc** | 149 **77** | | | | |
| **ei** | 129 **55** | **ng** | 149 **77** | | | **w** | 149 |
| **eu** | 129 | **nn** | 138-139 147 | | | | |
| | | | | | | **x** | 149 |
| **f** | 146 **73** | **o** | 116-117 122-128 **31 32** | | | | |
| **ff** | 138-139 146 | **oi** | 125 129 **58** | | | **y** | 149 |
| | | | | | | | |
| **g** | 138 140-141 **72** | **p** | 138 142 **67 68** | | | **z** | 145 **81** |
| **ge** | 141 | **pp** | 138-139 | | | **zz** | 138-139 145 **81** |

*Dictionaries*

**Hoare, Alfred**   1952   A Short Italian Dictionary. Cambridge University Press (Italian-English)

**Garzanti**   1963   Dizionario Garzanti. Milano: Garzanti Editori (Italian only) Now available in paper-back.

**Hazon, Mario**   1973   Dizionario inglese-italiano, italiano-inglese. Edizione pratica scolastica. Milano: Garzanti Editori. A truly excellent but expensive dictionary with many listings. Hard cover only.

**Mestica, Enrico**   1959   Dizionario della lingua italiana. Torino: S. Lattes & Co. (Italian only)

Many Italian-English dictionaries do not indicate pronunciation. The more reliable ones (such as those noted above) do not give a complete phonetic rendering of each word because Italian is a nearly phonetic language with few variables in pronunciation.

In these four dictionaries a grave accent is used to indicate stressed open **e** and **o** (**è, ò**), an acute accent to indicate stressed closed **e** and **o** (**é, ó**). In conversational Italian it is assumed that unstressed **e** and **o** are closed.

Hoare uses a dot over **z** to indicate that it is voiced (**ż**). Garzanti uses z for unvoiced **z** and ʒ for voiced **z**. Hazon does not indicate voiced or unvoiced **z**.

While not ideal, Hoare seems to be the best all-round Italian-English dictionary. Garzanti, unfortunately in Italian only, has many more separate word listings, including verb forms. A practical procedure is to use the Hoare, Hazon or Cassell for translating and Garzanti for pronunciation.

The *Cassell Italian-English Dictionary*, which is widely available, has many listings but is not very helpful in pronunciation. Many cases of stressed **e** and **o** are not indicated as open or closed, and the rendering of voiced and unvoiced **z** is not in agreement with other dictionaries.

*110 Italian*

*Syllabification*

The first step in pronouncing Italian is the dividing of words into syllables.

1   A single consonant between two vowels goes with the second.
    **ma-ri-to      po-te-re**

2   Double consonants are split between syllables.
    **el-la      som-mo**

3   Two consonants, the first of which is **l,m,n,r** are split between syllables.
    **al-to      an-ti-co**

4   Otherwise, two consonants remain together in the second syllable.
    **giu-sto      fi-glio**

5   Three consonants divide one plus two
    **com-pro      al-tro**

    except for **s**, which joins the second syllable.
    **a-stro      mo-stra**

1   Most commonly the stress in Italian occurs on the penultimate
    (next to last) syllable.
    **bẹ-ne    ạl-tro**

2   Some words are stressed on the final syllable. When the stress
    occurs there, it is always indicated by an accent mark. The direction
    of that mark has no significance: sometimes an acute is used, but
    more often a grave.
    **cit-tạ̀    di-le-guọ̀    par-lọ̀**

3   Some words are stressed on the anti-penultimate syllable (third
    from the end). This stress is not indicated by an accent mark. It
    can usually be determined by looking the word up in a dictionary
    or by reciting the text aloud in the rhythm of its musical setting.
    **cẹ-ne-re    pạr-la-no**

## VOWELS

Italian has seven, and only seven, vowel sounds.
Some Italian dialects have more, but they should not
be used in pronunciation on the stage.

Chart of Italian vowels, showing relative height, roundness, opening and closure.

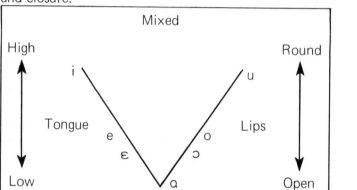

On the chart in Part 1 Italian closed **e** and **o** are notated as [e²] and [o²] to indicate that they are lower (more open) than their counterparts in French and German. To avoid an overly complicated notation here they are transcribed simply as [e] and [o].

*Constant vowels*
   **a, i, u**

No matter where they are found, **a**, **i** and **u** are always pronounced with the same sounds.

**a** [ɑ]  is roughly equivalent to the **a** in English **father**, pronounced with relaxed lips and dropped jaw.
**lana    sala    canta    forza    Aida**

American singers need to be especially careful not to allow a final **a** to drop into the obscure vowel sound used in pronouncing the name **Rita** in English.

**i** [i]  is equivalent to the vowel in English **meet**.
**infinito    fino    impare    limpida    ira    infidi**

It is never pronounced as in English **infinite**.

**u** [u]  is equivalent to the vowel in English **moon**.
**futura    muta    tutto    turbato    lunga    giunto**

It is never pronounced as in English **foot** or **sure**.

**e** and **o** each have a closed and an open sound.

Open **e** [ɛ]   is equivalent to English **bed** and **sent**.
**bello**   **senso**   **letto**   **gemma**   **lento**

Open **o** [ɔ]   is equivalent to English **cough**. For this sound the jaw is dropped
and the corners of the mouth brought in slightly.
**forza**   **gioio**   **gioco**   **porta**   **gobbo**

Closed **e** [e]   has no true equivalent in English, but it closely approaches the very
first vowel in English **chaotic**. It is also approximated by the vowel
in **day** when pronounced with an Irish brogue.
**vero**   **seno**   **stella**   **velo**   **sera**   **catena**

Closed **o** [o]   also has no true equivalent in English, but it closely approaches the
very first vowel in English **rowing**. It is also approximated by the
vowel in **go** when pronounced with an Irish brogue.
**solo**   **sono**   **molta**   **voce**   **dolce**   **romba**

The closed **e** and **o** in Italian are rarely followed by a diphthong
glide. In order to avoid an unwanted glide do not move tongue or
lips for the duration of the vowel.

Unstressed **e** and **o**   The pronunciation of unstressed **e** and **o** is not indicated in the
dictionaries. It is assumed that unstressed **e** and **o** are always closed
in spoken Italian. The modern vocal usage, however, makes variations
on this rule. Unstressed vowels seem to keep their height (their
closure, their tension) before the stressed syllable, perhaps even in
anticipation of it. The stress (which is quite strong in Italian) then
seems to release the tension in the word, causing subsequent vowels
to relax and open. From these observations, we may postulate the
rules following.

Like English, but unlike French and German, Italian has no "official"
stage diction. The following rules for unstressed **e** and **o** are arbitrary—
merely an attempt to codify the current Italian usage.
*116 Italian*

*Unstressed* **e** *and* **o**

Preceding the stress    unstressed **e** and **o** are closed.

[e]   **ve-ni̯-re**    **se-gui̯-ta**    **de-li̯-zia**    **fe-li̯-ce**    **spe-ran̯-za**

[o]   **do-ma̯-ni**    **so-spi̯-ra**    **com-pra̯-re**    **vo-la̯-re**

Following the stress
or final    unstressed **e** and **o** are open.

[ɛ]   **ve-nu̯-te**    **se-gui̯-te**    **de-li̯-zie**    **spie-ta̯-te**    **pen-sa̯-re**
       **o̯-pe-ra**    **an̯-ge-lo**    **te̯-ne-re**    **te̯-ne-bre**    **bat̯-te-re**
       **se**           **le**          **finchè**    **vendè**

[ɔ]   **la̯-dro**    **so-spi̯-ro**    **com-pra̯-to**    **pu̯-ro**    **sa̯-no**
       **co̯-mo-do**    **po̯-po-lo**    **ri-co̯-ve-ro**    **im-me̯-mo-re**
       **no**           **avrò**       **so**

In the examples following, pronunciation and stress are indicated
as in dictionaries:
an acute accent ( ´ ) = a closed vowel
a grave accent ( ` ) = an open vowel

Stressed **e** occurs in four positions:
1 ending a syllable
2 preceding a single consonant in the same syllable
3 preceding a double consonant
4 preceding a vowel

**1** Ending a syllable

Stressed **e**

1 is generally closed.

| | | | | |
|---|---|---|---|---|
| mé-no | pé-na | vé-ro | po-té-re | vo-lé-re |
| mé-glio | sé-ra | sé-gno | ve-dé-re | di-sdé-gno |

2 is open when it occurs in a stressed ante-penult.

| | | | |
|---|---|---|---|
| sè-co-lo | mè-di-co | Cè-sa-re | im-mè-mo-re |
| gè-li-da | tè-ne-ro | tè-ne-bra | cè-de-re |

3 is open when preceded by **i** or **u**.

| | | | |
|---|---|---|---|
| piè-no | ciè-lo | ciè-co | liè-to |
| iè-ri | diè-tro | guèr-ra | guèl-fo |

4 is open when followed by **s** plus another consonant.

| | | | |
|---|---|---|---|
| è-sco | tem-pè-sta | fu-nè-sto | dè-stra |
| mè-sto | pè-sco | vè-spa | pè-ste |

5 is open in the suffix **-ero** in words of more than two syllables.

| | | | |
|---|---|---|---|
| mi-stè-ro | se-vè-ro | im-pè-ro | mi-ni-stè-ro |
| sin-cè-ro | al-tè-ro | bo-lè-ro | ma-gi-stè-ro |

6 is usually open when followed by a consonant and a glide.

| | | | |
|---|---|---|---|
| sè-rio | gè-nio | nè-nia | tè-dio |
| in-gè-nua | tèm-pio | | |

occasionally closed

| | | |
|---|---|---|
| tré-gua | ém-pio | e-sém-pio |

**2** Preceding a consonant
in the same syllable    stressed **e**

1    is generally open.

| | | | |
|---|---|---|---|
| **sèm-pre** | **sèn-to** | **pèn-so** | **svèl-to** |
| **cèr-to** | **sèn-so** | **sèm-pli-ce** | **a-pèr-to** |

2    is always closed in the following suffixes:

Nouns:    -éccio, -éccia    **fréccia, bréccia**
          -éggio, -éggia    **paréggio, tréggia**
          -éssa             **contéssa, principéssa**
          -ézza             **bellézza, debolézza**
          -éfice            **carnéfice, benéfice**

Adverbs:  -ménte            **francaménte**
          -évole            **piacévole**

Verbs:    -émmo             **avémmo**
          -ésse, -éssi      **avésse, avéssi**
          -ésso, -éssa      **promésso, riméssa**
          -évano            **credévano**
          -érono            **credérono**
          -éssero           **credéssero**
          -éssimo           **credéssimo**

3    is closed in diminutives ending in **-etto** (**-etta, -etti, -ette**).

| | | |
|---|---|---|
| **cerchiétto** | **casétta** | **donnétta** |
| **poverétti** | **barchétte** | **canzonétte** |
| **Rigolétto** | **Violétta** | **Musétta** |

4    is closed in non-diminutives ending in **-etto** (**-etta, -etti, -ette**)
     when from a Latin root spelled with **i**.

| | | | |
|---|---|---|---|
| **détto** | **benedétto** | **strétta** | **vendétta** |

5   is open when from a Latin root spelled with **e**.

| | | | |
|---|---|---|---|
| **accètto** | **affètto** | **aspètto** | **dilètto** |
| **oggètto** | **perfètto** | **pètto** | **soggètto** |

Extensive knowledge of Latin is not necessary to apply the rules, for many English cognates preserve the Latin vowel: **dictum** (**dicto = détto**), **strict** (**stricto = strétta**), **vindictive** (**vindicta = vendétta**), **object** (**objecto = oggètto**), **pectoral** (**pectora = pètto**). If the word ending in **-etto**, (**-etta**, **-etti** or **-ette**) is not a diminutive or the English cognate does not come to mind, check the dictionary for whether **e** is closed or open.

**3 Preceding a double consonant**   stressed **e** is sometimes open, sometimes closed.

| *open* | *closed* |
|---|---|
| **fèbbre** | **nébbia** |
| **ècco** | **sécco** |
| **règge** | **gréggio** |
| **bèlla** | **stélla** |
| **adèsso** | **stésso** |

As stressed **e** before a double consonant is unpredictable, it is necessary to check each case in a dictionary.

**4 Preceding a vowel**   stressed **e**

1   is usually open.

**lèi**    **sèi**    **bèi**    **rèa**    **idèa**    **dèa**

2   in poetic Italian, the third person singular and plural of the imperfect tense may undergo a contraction.

**paréva = paréa**      **lucévano = lucéano**

In such cases the stressed **e** is closed, as it would be in the non-contracted forms.

| | | |
|---|---|---|
| **tacéa** | **ridéa** | **piangéa** |
| **tacéan** | **ridéan** | **piangéan** |

*Stressed* o

Stressed **o** occurs in four positions:
1 ending a syllable
2 preceding a single consonant in the same syllable
3 preceding a double consonant
4 preceding a vowel

**1** Ending a syllable    stressed **o**

1    is generally closed.

| | | | | |
|---|---|---|---|---|
| **só-no** | **vó-ce** | **dó-no** | **cró-ce** | **a-mó-re** |
| **ó-ra** | **nó-me** | **gó-la** | **pó-sto** | **vó-lo** |

2    is open in a stressed ante-penult.

| | | | |
|---|---|---|---|
| **pò-ve-ro** | **òt-ti-mo** | **nò-bi-le** | **ò-pe-ra** |
| **mò-bi-le** | **cò-mo-do** | **pò-po-lo** | **lò-gi-co** |

3    is open when preceded by **i** or **u**.

| | | | |
|---|---|---|---|
| **piò-ve** | **chiò-ma** | **fiò-co** | **viò-le** |
| **cuò-co** | **buò-no** | **vuò-le** | **duò-lo** |

Some words having the stressed **uo** combination may be spelled without the **u**. In such cases the **o** must still be pronounced open.

| | | | | | |
|---|---|---|---|---|---|
| **cuò-re** | = | **cò-re** | **muò-ve** | = | **mò-ve** |
| **fuò-co** | = | **fò-co** | **nuò-vo** | = | **nò-vo** |
| **giuò-co** | = | **giò-co** | **scuò-la** | = | **scò-la** |
| **luò-go** | = | **lò-go** = **lò-co** | **suò-na** | = | **sò-na** |
| **muò-re** | = | **mò-re** | **u-si-gnuò-lo** | = | **u-si-gnò-lo** |

4　is open when followed by **gli**.
　　**fò-glio**　　**vò-glio**　　**sò-glio**　　　**or-gò-glio**

5　is open when followed by one or more consonants plus a glide.
　　**stò-ria**　　**glò-ria**　　**ò-dio**　　**prò-prio**
　　**peò-nia**　　**vit-tò-ria**　**Tò-nio**　　**me-mò-ria**

6　is open in the noun ending **-òro** and its plural **-òri**.
　　**òro**　　　**tesòro**　　**ristòro**
　　**tesòri**　　**Alidòro**　　**Lindòro**

7　is always closed in the endings **-óso** (**-ósa**, **-ósi**, **-óse**) and **-óne**
　(and its plural **-óni**), even when preceded by **i** or **u**.
　　**amoróso**　　**doloróso**　　**graziósa**　　**malizióse**
　　**cannóne**　　**ragióne**　　**nazióni**　　**religióni**

8　is closed in the ending **-óre** and its plural **-óri**, unless preceded by **u**.
　　**amóre**　　**dottóre**　　**maggióri**　　**fióri**

but　**cuòre**, **fuòri**, etc. are pronounced with open **o**.

**2** Preceding a consonant
in the same syllable   stressed **o**

1   is generally open.

| | | | |
|---|---|---|---|
| **mòr-te** | **fòr-za** | **pòr-ta** | **sòr-te** |
| **còr-po** | **sòl-di** | **pòr-gi** | **ri-sòl-ve** |

2   followed by **l** plus **c**, **f**, **g**, **m**, **p** or **t** is closed.

| | | | |
|---|---|---|---|
| **dól-ce** | **gól-fo** | **vól-go** | **a-scól-to** |
| **cól-mo** | **cól-pa** | **vól-to** | **a-scól-ta-no** |

Exception   **vòlta** (**vault**, **arch**, or **turn**).

3   followed by **mb**, **mm** or **mp** is closed.

| | | | |
|---|---|---|---|
| **óm-bra** | **sóm-mo** | **tróm-ba** | **róm-pa** |
| **bóm-ba** | **co-lóm-ba** | **pióm-ba** | **róm-pe-re** |

Note that in **rómpere** (and in words like it) the **o** is closed even
though followed by a consonant in the same syllable, and stressed
on the ante-penult.

4   followed by a single **n** in the same syllable is closed.

| | | | |
|---|---|---|---|
| **cón** | **cón-te** | **cón-tro** | **fón-do** |
| **món-do** | **pón-te** | **rón-di-ne** | **fón-de-re** |

Note, therefore, that **róndine** and **fóndere** (and other similar
words) are pronounced with a closed **o**, even though stressed on
the ante-penult.

This rule does not apply when stressed **o** is followed by double **n**.
In such cases, the **o** may be closed or open.
**dònna** [ɔ]   **gònna** [ɔ]   **nònno** [ɔ]   **sónno** [o]

5 followed by **s** plus one or more consonants is often open

| | | | |
|---|---|---|---|
| **bò-sco** | **cò-sta** | **fòs-sa** | **in-chiò-stro** |
| **mòs-sa** | **nò-stro** | **ò-spi-te** | **òs-so** |
| **pò-sta** | **tò-sto** | **sò-sta** | |

but occasionally closed.

| | | | | |
|---|---|---|---|---|
| **mó-stro** | **mó-sca** | **fó-sco** | **ló-sco** | **pó-sto** |

**3** Preceding a double consonant

stressed **o** is sometimes open, sometimes closed.

| *open* | *closed* |
|---|---|
| **ròcco** | **bócca** |
| **zòlla** | **bólla** |
| **dònna** | **sónno** |
| **còppia** | **dóppio** |
| **còtto** | **rótto** |

As stressed **o** followed by a double consonant is unpredictable, it is necessary to check each case in a dictionary.

**4** Preceding a vowel

stressed **o** is usually open, sometimes closed.

| *open* | *closed* |
|---|---|
| **pòi** | **nói** |
| **vuòi** | **vói** |
| **tuòi** | |
| **suòi** | |

*Contraction and apocopation*

Contraction      As the preposition **con** is pronounced with closed **o**, so are the contractions **cól, cólla, cói, cólle**.

The contraction **nól** (**non** + **il**) is also pronounced with closed **o**.

Apocopation      (**troncamento**) is the process of omitting the final vowel from an Italian word. It is easy to recognize because most Italian words end in vowels. Only a few prepositions (**con**, **per**, etc.) and the negative **non** end in consonants. All common nouns, verbs, adjectives and adverbs end in vowels.

Apocopation does not change the pronunciation of a shortened word. In **sóno** [so nɔ], for example, the stressed **o** remains closed if the final **o** is dropped. [son] not [sɔn].

| | | | | |
|---|---|---|---|---|
| **me-no** | [me nɔ] | = | **men** | [men] |
| **cuo-re** | [kwɔ rɛ] | = | **cuor** | [kwɔr] or **cor** [kɔr] |
| **an-co-ra** | [aŋ ko rɑ] | = | **ancor** | [aŋ kor] |
| **pie-no** | [pjɛ nɔ] | = | **pien** | [pjɛn] |
| **mag-gio-re** | [mɑd:ʒo rɛ] | = | **maggior** | [mɑd:ʒor] |
| **ra-gio-ne** | [rɑ dʒo nɛ] | = | **ragion** | [rɑ dʒon] |

Although the rules quoted here cover the most troublesome cases of stressed **e** and **o**, there are many words in Italian which do not fit neatly into the preceding categories. The rules will serve as a guide, but it is necessary to use a good pronouncing Italian dictionary constantly. This is not such a chore as it initially might seem, for Italian librettists and poets tend to use many of the same words over and over.

Here are a few of the most common exceptions which occur in many texts.

| | | | |
|---|---|---|---|
| **be-ne** | [bɛ nɛ] | | |
| **bre-ve** | [brɛ vɛ] | **pre-go** | [prɛ gɔ] |
| **co-sa** | [kɔ zɑ] | **ro-sa** | [rɔ zɑ] |
| **e** | [e] | **spe-me** | [spɛ mɛ] |
| **è** | [ɛ] | **spo-sa** | [spɔ zɑ] |
| **po-co** | [pɔ kɔ] | **spo-so** | [spɔ zɔ] |
| **po-sa** | [pɔ zɑ] | **vol-ta** | [vɔl tɑ] |

**e-ro, e-ri, e-ra**   [ɛrɔ], [ɛri], [ɛrɑ]

According to predominant vocal (but not conversational) usage, the following are pronounced with open **e**:

| | | | |
|---|---|---|---|
| **del** | **dello** | **della** | **delle** |
| **nel** | **nello** | **nella** | **nelle** |
| **questo** | **questa** | **questi** | **queste** |
| **quel** | **quello** | **quella** | **quelle** |
| **ella** | | | |

*Summary of stressed* **e** *and* **o**

|  | CLOSE | OPEN |

**e** ending a stressed syllable
unless

1 the stress occurs on the antepenult
2 it is preceded by **i** or **u**
3 it precedes **s** plus a consonant
4 it occurs in the ending **-ero** in words
   of more than two syllables
5 it is followed by a consonant and a glide

Stressed **e** followed by a vowel or consonant
in the same syllable
except

Certain endings are always closed
(See the list on page 119)

Stressed **e** before a double consonant ⟷ Stressed **e** before a double consonant

Stressed **e** before a vowel

---

                CLOSE      OPEN

**o** ending a stressed syllable
unless

1 the stress occurs on the antepenult
2 it is preceded by **i** or **u**
3 it precedes **gli**
4 it precedes one or more consonants plus a glide
5 it precedes **s** plus a consonant (sometimes).

The ending **-óso** (- **ósa**, etc.)    The noun ending **-òro**
The ending **-óne** (- **óni**)    The ending **-uòre** (**-uòri**)
The ending **-óre** (**-óri** )

Stressed **o** followed by a consonant
in the same syllable
unless

1 preceding **l** + **c**, **f**, **g**, **m**, **p** or **t**
2 preceding **mb**, **mm** or **mp**
3 preceding single **n** in the same syllable

Stressed **o** before a double consonant ⟷ Stressed **o** before a double consonant

Stressed **o** before a vowel ⟷ Stressed **o** before a vowel
*128 Italian*

DIPHTHONGS

The four most common Italian diphthongs are:

**ai** [ɑ:i]  **mai**     **sai**     **vai**

**au** [ɑ:u]  **aura**    **pausa**   **Lauretta**

**ei** [ɛ:i]  **lei**     **nei**     **sei**

**oi** [ɔ:i]  **poi**     **vuoi**    **suoi**

Diphthong combinations may also be found with:

**ae** [a:e]  **paesano**

**ao** [a:o]  **Paolo**    **ciao**

**eu** [e:u]  **feudale**   **Euridice**

In singing these diphthongs, the first of the two vowels must be lengthened in order to avoid making the second vowel seem like a separate syllable. Thus, if **mai** is to be sustained for four beats, the [i] part of the diphthong should not be sounded until after the second half of the fourth beat.

Sometimes a composer divides a diphthong into two separate notes (e.g. the first line of **Tu lo sai**). In such a case, the rhythmic intentions of the composer must be observed.

*129 Italian*

## GLIDES

A glide is an unstressed vowel which proceeds quickly and smoothly to a following vowel.

Italian has three:

| | | | | |
|---|---|---|---|---|
| [j] | **pianto** | **pietà** | **fiore** | **fiume** |
| [w] | **guardo** | **questo** | **squilla** | **suono** |
| [ʎ] | **gli** | **gl'angeli** | **aglio** | **gl'occhi** |

In older spellings, [j] may be spelled as **j**.
**gioja = gioia**                    **muojo = muoio**

**i** is often used to soften a preceding **c** or **g**. In such a case, the **i** is not to be considered a glide or vowel and is silent.
**cielo**          **ciao**          **Giovanni**      **lasciate**

If no vowel follows the **i**, it is, of course, sounded.
**cinto**          **ciglio**        **giro**          **Gilda**

The four (or seven) common diphthongs may be recognized from their spelling: **ai, au, ei, oi (ae, ao, eu)**.

The glide [ʎ] may be recognized from its spelling: **gli**.

The vowel combinations **i** plus a vowel, and **u** plus a vowel most often indicate glides. At other times, however, they are treated like diphthongs (long first vowel, short second vowel).

1  If an accent occurs on the second vowel, the combination is a glide.
   **più** [pju]   **piè** [pjɛ]   **odiò** [o djɔ]   **seguì** [se gwi]
   **diè** [djɛ]   **può** [pwɔ]   **Liù** [lju]   **dileguò** [di le gwɔ]

   In **ciò** and **già** there is no glide. The **i** is silent after **c** and **g**.

   **Qua** and **qui** have glides because **qu** in Italian is always pronounced [kw].

2  If no accent occurs on the second vowel in a monosyllable, the combination is a diphthong.
   **io**  [i:ɔ]    **fia** [fi:a]   **rio** [ri:ɔ]   **sue** [su:ɛ]
   **dio** [di:ɔ]   **zio** [tsi:ɔ]  **via** [vi:a]   **cui** [ku:i]
   **mio** [mi:ɔ]   **reo** [rɛ:ɔ]   **lui** [lu:i]   **due** [du:ɛ]
   **sia** [si:a]   **pio** [pi:ɔ]   **tuo** [tu:ɔ]   **fui** [fu:i]

   N. B. A colon after a phonetic symbol indicates that the sound should be lengthened.

3  In polysyllabic words ending in these vowel combinations, if the final syllable is unstressed, it will have a glide.
   **aria**  [a rja]   **Canio** [ka njɔ]   **segue** [se gwɛ]
   **rabbia** [rab:bja]   **smanie** [zma njɛ]   **statua** [sta twa]

4    In polysyllabic words with no accent mark, if the stress falls on the
     final syllable, the vowel combination will be treated as a diphthong.
     **poesia** [po e zi:ɑ]    **malia** [mɑ li:ɑ]    **bramosia** [brɑ mo zi:ɑ]
     **polizia** [po li tsi:ɑ]    **natio** [nɑ ti:ɔ]    **signoria**  [si ɲo ri:ɑ]

5    In the interior of a word, **i** or **u** followed by another vowel will always
     produce a glide.
     **piacer**    [pjɑ tʃer]    **chioma** [kjɔ mɑ]    **chiuso** [kju zo]
     **pianto**    [pjɑn tɔ]    **siete**    [sjɛ tɛ]    **buono** [bwɔ nɔ]
     **guardare** [gwɑr dɑ rɛ]    **guisa**    [gwi zɑ]

6    The third person plural verb ending **-ano** is always unstressed.
     **siano** [si:ɑnɔ]    **stiano** [sti:ɑnɔ]    **fiano** [fi:ɑnɔ] *etc.*

*Singing diphthongs*

Italian grammarians have yet to agree on whether words like **io**, **mio**, **via**, etc. are monosyllabic diphthongs, or whether they are words of two syllables. When these words are set to two notes, there is no question. Often, however, composers set them to a single note. In such cases they may be executed in several ways:

1   They may be sung like true diphthongs—that is, by lengthing the first vowel as long as possible, treating the second vowel as a glide-off (tucking it in at the very end of the note).

2   For short or moderate note values, half of the value is given to the first vowel and half to the second.

$$\text{io} \;=\; \text{i - o} \qquad\qquad \text{mia} \;=\; \text{mi - a}$$

Care must be taken to go smoothly from the first vowel to the second. The result must not sound like two notes.

3   Notes of long duration permit greater latitude.

$$\text{io} \;=\; \text{i - o} \quad or \quad \text{i - o} \quad or\ even \quad \text{i - o} \;\;\text{(if the word begins on a strong beat)}$$

*Elision*

Italian words are often linked together in such a way that two or more vowels may fall together on the same note. The division of time values between the vowels varies greatly from performer to performer, but there are three rules of thumb which may be helpful:

1  A stressed vowel should last longer than an unstressed one.

2  When choosing among vowels occurring in unstressed syllables, the vowel belonging to the more important word will be of longer duration. When judging importance, rate a verb, for example, as more important than an article. In the succession **sono un**, therefore, the **o** would be held longer than the **u**, giving the effect of a diphthong.

3  When in doubt divide the note value equally between the vowels. This procedure has the added value of greater clarity of vowel sounds. In such a division, be sure to go smoothly from one vowel to the next. The effect should not be of two or three separate notes, but of one note with changing vowels.

l'a-ria è an-cor = l'a-ria è an-cor

## CONSONANTS

Italian consonants may be single (as in **grato**), or they may be double (as in **gratto**).

A single consonant is pronounced with the vowel that follows it. A vowel preceding a single consonant must continue to sound until the consonant is articulated.

$$\text{\musHalfNote} \quad \text{\musHalfNote}$$

gra ⟶ to

If the vowel does stop, however briefly, the single **t** will sound like a double **tt**, and the meaning of the word in this example will be **scratch** instead of **grateful**. Vowels occurring before single consonants must be extended as long as possible.

Vowels before double consonants are shortened, so that the double sound may be prolonged energetically. This variation in vowel length (long before single consonants, short before double consonants) greatly influences the rhythm of spoken Italian and has a great effect on the flavor of the sung language.

Double consonants divide into two groups, *stop* consonants and
*continuing* consonants.

Stop consonants
**bb**, **cc**, **dd**, **gg**, **pp**, **tt** and **zz**.

With these the breath actually stops momentarily while
the consonant sound is held in suspension.

| | | | | | |
|---|---|---|---|---|---|
| **rabbia** | [rɑb:bjɑ] | **faccia** | [fɑt:ʃɑ] | **vacca** | [vɑk:kɑ] |
| **freddo** | [fred:dɔ] | **peggio** | [pɛd:ʒɔ] | **aggrave** | [ɑg:grɑvɛ] |
| **scoppio** | [skɔp:pjɔ] | **donnetta** | [don:net:tɑ] | **pizza** | [pit:sɑ] |

A similar phenomenon occurs in English, but not within words. It
happens between words. The following pairs without separations
between the words exemplify the principle:

**Bob bakes**   **Rick cares**   **Meg goes**   **Hap plays**   **Pat tries**

The consonants **b**, **p**, **d**, **t**, **k** and **g** are dry in Italian.

In the English **paw**, there is a little puff of air inserted between the
consonant and the vowel. In Italian **po'**, there is no similar inter-
ruption between the consonant and the vowel sounds. The same
difference may be observed by comparing the words **car** and **casa**,
**two** and **tu**.

Continuing consonants
**ff**, **ll**, **mm**, **nn**, **rr**, **ss** and **vv**.

With these the breath does not stop flowing. In those continuing
consonants which are voiced, the pitch is maintained.

| | | | | | | |
|---|---|---|---|---|---|---|
| Voiced: | **bella** | [bɛl:lɑ] | **sommi** | [som:mi] | **anno** | [ɑn:nɔ] |
| | **orror** | [or:ror] | **avvenir** | [ɑv:ve nir] | | |
| Unvoiced: | **tuffare** | [tuf:fɑ rɛ] | **lasso** | [lɑs:sɔ] | | |

Again, parallels may be made with English.

| Compare | **if few** | with | **if you** |
|---|---|---|---|
| | **Tim mixes** | | **timid** |
| | **Ann knows** | | **an odor** |
| | **pass sober** | | **pass over** |

A double consonant may never be shortened to a single consonant, even in rapid tempo, because the meaning could be changed drastically.

| | | | |
|---|---|---|---|
| **carro** cart | **caro** dear |
| **ecco** here | **eco** echo |
| **fatto** done, a fact | **fato** fate |
| **faccie** faces | **face** torch |
| **mamma** mother | **m'ama** loves me |
| **notte** night | **note** notes |
| **vanno** they go | **vano** vain |
| **ville** villas | **vile** cowardly |
| **anno** year | **ano** anus |

When, in a word group, a monosyllabic word precedes a word beginning with a consonant, this consonant may be prolonged as if it were double. Such doubling is not possible after articles, personal pronouns or the preposition **di**.

**a Roma**    [ɑr:romɑ]
**chi sa**    [kis:sɑ]
**più caro**  [pjuk:kɑrɔ]

This doubling of initial consonants is more commonly practiced in central and southern Italy than in the north. In order to avoid a conflict with the basically legato style of Italian singing, initial doubling should not be applied indiscriminately in singing, but should be reserved for emotional phrases, or phrases in a *quasi-parlando* style.

In the examples following, as before, vowels and stress are indicated by an acute accent ( ´ ) signifying a closed vowel; a grave accent ( ` ) signifying an open vowel.

**c** and **g** are hard  [k] and [g] when they occur before **a**, **o**, **u**, and consonants (including **h**). In Italian  there is no puff of air inserted between [k] and a vowel following it.

| | | |
|---|---|---|
| cá-ra | cò-sa | cú-ra |
| che | cró-ce | clí-ma |
| gá-la | gó-la | guár-da |
| gher-mí-ta | grán-de | Re-spí-ghi |

| | | | |
|---|---|---|---|
| a-cán-to | ac-cán-to | ma-gá-ri | ag-grá-do |
| è-co | èc-co | le-gá-to | ag-gán-cio |
| fí-chi | fíc-chi | a-go-nía | ag-gre-dí-re |
| pò-ca | ròc-ca | fú-ga | fúg-ga |
| Lu-cá-no | Lúc-ca | u-guá-le | ag-guá-to |

**c** and **g** remain hard  before **a**, **o**, **u** and consonants when they are preceded by **s**.

| | |
|---|---|
| **scocco** [skɔk:kɔ] | **scherno** [sker nɔ] |
| **sgarra** [zgɑr:rɑ] | **sgherri** [zgɛr:ri] |

| | | | |
|---|---|---|---|
| scám-pa | scò-la | scú-sa | schiè-na |
| scá-la | na-scón-do | scú-ro | schiòp-po |
| sgóm-bra | sgón-fio | scrí-ve | Schíc-chi |

**c** and **g** are soft when they occur before **e** or **i**.

**c** before **e** or **i**   sounds like the **ch** in English **church**. [tʃ]
**cce** or **cci**   is executed by prolonging the [t] part of the sound. [t:ʃ]
**bacio** [bɑ tʃɔ]     **taccio** [tɑ t:ʃɔ]

**g** before **e** or **i**   sounds like the **g** in the English name **George**. [dʒ]
**gge** or **ggi**   is executed by holding the [d] before releasing the [ʒ].
**giungere** [dʒun dʒɛ rɛ]    **raggio** [rɑ d:ʒɔ]

**i** is silent when it follows **c** or **g** unless there is no other vowel. It
sounds in **cibo** and **giro**, but not in **bacio** or **raggio**.

| | | | |
|---|---|---|---|
| cé-ne-re | cí-glio | gèn-te | giar-dí-no |
| bá-cio | fác-cio | má-gi | mág-gi |
| fé-ce | bréc-cie | re-gí-na | règ-gia |
| fe-lí-ci | Ríc-ci | ví-ge | fíg-ge |
| góc-ce | vó-ce | dò-ge | lòg-gia |
| uc-cèl-lo | lu-cèn-te | bu-gía | fug-gía |

**s** before **ce** or **ci**   produces the sound [ʃ], as in the English **shoe**. **la-scia-te** [lɑ ʃɑ tɛ]

| | | | |
|---|---|---|---|
| scè-na | scé-so | scé-mo | af-fa-sci-ná-to |
| scia-gú-ra | lá-sci | sciá-bla | pò-scia |

**s** before **ge** or **gi**   does not affect the sound of soft **g**.
**sge-lo** [zdʒɛ lɔ]     **di-sgiun-to** [di zdʒun tɔ]

dry **b**    [b] must have a definite pitch; this pitch makes it a *voiced* consonant.

dry **p**

| | | |
|---|---|---|
| **pón-te** | **piè-de** | **píc-co-lo** |
| **pò-po-lo** | **po-po-ló-so** | **pióm-ba** |
| **bál-lo** | **bá-da** | **bèl-lo** |
| **bóm-ba** | **bab-buí-no** | **bóc-ca** |

| | | | |
|---|---|---|---|
| **bá-ba** | **báb-bo** | **pá-pa** | **páp-po** |
| **è-ba-no** | **èb-be-ro** | **se-pá-ra** | **sèp-pi** |
| **dé-bo-le** | **déb-bio** | **è-po-ca** | **ép-pu-re** |
| **lò-bo** | **gòb-bo** | **dó-po** | **dóp-pio** |
| **dú-bi-to** | **dúb-bio** | **lú-po** | **grúp-po** |

**d**    In addition to being dry (no air between consonant and the following
**t**    vowel), these consonants are also dental. In Italian, the tip of the
tongue is touched against the back of the upper teeth for **d** and **t**.

| | | | | |
|---|---|---|---|---|
| **dó-ve** | **fréd-do** | **dán-do-la** | **dèn-ti** | **ld-dío** |
| **tán-to** | **tèn-de-re** | **di-lèt-to** | **tút-ti** | **af-fèt-ti** |

| | | | |
|---|---|---|---|
| **rá-do** | **rad-dóp-pio** | **fá-to** | **fát-to** |
| **vé-do** | **Néd-da** | **ché-to** | **schiét-to** |
| **ra-dí-ce** | **ad-dío** | **fá-ti** | **fát-ti** |
| **brò-do** | **bòd-da** | **mò-ta** | **mòt-ta** |
| **sú-di-cio** | **súd-di-to** | **ú-ti-le** | **dút-ti-le** |

**st**    Special care should be taken with **t** when it follows **s**. In English,
**s** and **t** are produced with the tongue in the same position—against
the hard gum ridge. In Italian, the tongue must make a movement
forward to the teeth when going from **s** to **t**. This movement is
necessary and must be executed quickly or the **s** will lisp.

| | | | | |
|---|---|---|---|---|
| **sta** | **sto** | **stá-to** | **e-stá-te** | **e-stá-ti-co** |
| **stía** | **stú-fo** | **mè-sto** | **rè-sto** | **è-sta-si** |
| **á-stro** | **sté-so** | **tè-sta** | **stél-la** | **de-stí-no** |

s may be unvoiced [s], or voiced [z]:

unvoiced   when initial (except before a voiced consonant).
1   **sá-la**        **scuò-la**        **sfí-da**        **stá-to**

2   when followed by unvoiced consonants.
**a-scól-ta**    **di-sfí-do**    **a-spèt-to**

3   when preceded by consonant and followed by vowel.
**sèn-si**    **ór-so**        **pen-sá-re**

4   when doubled (it is also lengthened).
**tás-sa**    **més-sa**    **fís-so**    **fòs-sa**

voiced   when initial, before a voiced consonant.
1   **sbá-glio**    **sdé-gno**    **sguár-do**    **sleá-le**
**smá-nia**    **snèl-lo**    **sru-vi-dí-re**    **svá-go**

2   when interior, before a voiced consonant.
**di-sdé-gno**    **fan-tá-sma**    **me-dé-sma**

3   when between two vowels (intervocalic).
**rò-sa**    **spò-so**        **scé-sa**    **cò-sa**

**vá-so**    **tás-so**
**pré-sa**    **près-sa**
**físo**    **fís-so**
**pò-sa**    **pòs-sa**
**l'ú-so**    **lús-so**

*Summary of* s

Voiced **s**

  1  Single **s** between vowels  **rosa**

  2  Before a voiced consonant  **sdegno**
Remember this as the "Sdegno Rule".

Unvoiced **s**  All other cases

Exception  A single **s** occurring after the prefix **pre-** (when it means *before*), or after the prefix **ri-** (when it means *again*) must be unvoiced.

Thus, **presento** [pre sɛn tɔ] means **I anticipate**, or **I feel beforehand.** If pronounced [pre zɛn tɔ] it means **I present.**

Similarly, **risentire** (to feel again), **risalire** (to mount again), and **risuonare** (to play again) are all pronounced with unvoiced **s.**

**cosí**
**cosa**
**casa**  A number of exceptions to the rule of the intervocalic **s** are listed in Italian dictionaries and grammars. Many are theoretical and few of them are observed in practice. Those most commonly observed are **cosí** [ko si], **còsa** [kɔ sɑ], and **casa** [kɑ sɑ]. Quite often even these are spoken and sung with voiced **s.**

**sei**  The number **sei** (six) is pronounced with unvoiced **s** in compounds **ventisei**, **trentasei**, etc.

Reflexive **si**  In poetic Italian, the reflexive pronoun **si** may be placed after the verb. When in this position, verb and pronoun are written as one word. In these cases (which do not often occur), the **s** is unvoiced, as if it were initial.
**si sènte = sèntesi**    **si chiúde = chiúdesi**    **si párta = pártasi**

**z** may be voiced or unvoiced.

Unvoiced **z** is pronounced [ts] when single. For a double unvoiced **z**, the first part of the sound is prolonged (the **t** is held in suspension) [t:s].
**zúppa** [tsup:pɑ]     **fierézza** [fje ret:sɑ]

Voiced **z** is pronounced [dz] when single. For a double voiced **z**, the first part of the sound is prolonged (the **d** is held in suspension) [d:z].
**zónzo** [dzon dzɔ]     **mèzzo** [mɛd:zɔ]

Because **z** is so unpredictable, exact rules are difficult, if not impossible to formulate. Each case must be looked up in a dictionary.

**z** [ts] unvoiced is usual.
**zío**  [tsi:ɔ]       **zúc-che-ro** [tsuk:kɛ rɔ]    **zit-to**   [tsit:tɔ]
**sèn-za** [sɛn tsɑ]    **zín-ga-ro** [tsiŋ gɑ rɔ]     **a-ván-za** [ɑ vɑn tsɑ]
**zi-tèl-la** [tsi tɛl:lɑ]  **in-nán-zi**  [in:nɑn tsi]

**z** [dz] voiced is encountered occasionally.
**zè-nit**   [dzɛ nit]    **zè-ro**   [dzɛ rɔ]      **zòl-la** [dzɔl:lɑ]
**bón-zo**   [bon dzɔ]    **don-zèl-la** [don dzɛl:lɑ]
**zef-fi-rét-ti** [dzef:fi ret:ti]  **Do-ni-zét-ti** [do ni dzet:ti]

**zz** [t:s] is usually unvoiced. (The **t** is prolonged.)
**pèz-zo**   [pɛt:sɔ]     **póz-zo**   [pot:sɔ]      **píz-za** [pit:sɑ]
**páz-zo**   [pɑt:sɔ]     **piáz-za**   [pjɑt:sɑ]    **ráz-za** [rɑt:sɑ]
**ri-chéz-za** [ri ket:sɑ]   **bel-léz-za**  [bel:let:sɑ]
**San-túz-za** [sɑn tut:sɑ] **am-maz-zá-re** [ɑm:mɑt:sɑ rɛ]

**zz** [d:z] is occasionally voiced. (The **d** is prolonged.)
**mèz-zo**    [mɛd:zɔ]      **az-zúr-ro**   [ɑd:zur:rɔ]
**o-riz-zón-te** [o rid:zon tɛ]   **a-na-liz-zá-re** [ɑ nɑ lid:zɑ rɛ]

**f**   is pronounced as in English.

**fá-ma**       **fa-tá-le**       **fan-fá-ra**      **far-fa-lét-ta**

| | |
|---|---|
| **a-fá-to** | **af-fát-to** |
| **be-fá-na** | **bèf-fa** |
| **di-fèn-de-re** | **dif-fí-ci-le** |
| **mo-fé-ta** | **mof-fét-ta** |
| **tú-fo** | **túf-fo** |

**h**   is always silent.

**ho**    **ha**    **che**

**j**   occurs only in old spellings and is the glide [j].

**Já-go** [jɑ gɔ]     **re-jèt-ta** [re jɛt:tɑ]

**l**   is pronounced forward and is a dental consonant.

**láb-bro**    **lá-na**    **èl-la**    **stél-la**    **ól-tre**    **ál-tro**

| | |
|---|---|
| **pá-lo** | **bál-lo** |
| **té-la** | **bèl-la** |
| **vĭ-le** | **vĭl-le** |
| **fò-la** | **fòl-la** |
| **cu-lá-ta** | **cul-lá-ta** |

**m** is pronounced as in English.

má-le      mú-to          a-má-re          mám-mo-la          im-mèn-so

m'á-ma      mám-ma
gè-me       gèm-me
Mi-mí       dím-mi
pó-mo       sóm-mo
fú-mo       fúm-mo

**n** is dental (pronounced with the tip of the tongue against the back of the upper teeth). The dental **n** will be particularly useful in passages requiring rapid articulation.

nó-me      núl-la          nín-na-nán-na          nòn-na          in-no-cèn-te

fá-na        fán-no
pé-na        pén-na
di-nán-zi    in-nán-zi
dó-na        dòn-na
o-gnú-no     ca-lún-nia

r   in Italian is always either flipped or trilled. American **r** is never used.

[r:r]   Double **rr** is *always* trilled.

[r]   Single **r** between two vowels may *never* be trilled.

1

| | | | | |
|---|---|---|---|---|
| **vé-ro** | **né-ro** | **rá-ro** | **cú-ra** | **dú-ra** |
| **gĭ-ro** | **mĭ-ra** | **mo-ri-rò** | **mi-rá-re** | |
| **nar-rá-re** | **er-ró-re** | **or-ró-re** | **ter-ró-re** | |

When a single intervocalic **r** is trilled, a word of different meaning is often produced.

| | | |
|---|---|---|
| **cá-ro** | becomes | **cár-ro** |
| **è-ra** | | **èr-ra** |
| **ĭ-ra** | | **bĭr-ra** |
| **cò-re** | | **còr-re** |
| **pú-ro** | | **bur-ro** |

2   Initial **r**, or **r** in an initial consonant group may be trilled to increase intensity in words of strong emotional content.
**ráb-bia**     **cru-dè-le**     **strúg-go**     **in-grá-to**

3   **r** is a voiced consonant, and as such it must always have pitch. Even a single flip will sound clearly if properly voiced. A trilled **r** voiced will project better, and with less effort than an **r** without pitch.

**qu**     always sounds [kw].

**v**     sounds as in English.
**vá-no**          **vá-so**          **av-vám-pa**          **av-ve-ní-re**

**w, x** and **y**     occur only in foreign words. **w** is often pronounced [v].
**Wán-da**     **La Wál-ly** [la val:li]

**gn** [ɲ]     sounds the same as in French, in words like **agneau**. It is quite
similar to English **onion, pinion**, etc., except that the first syllable
of the English ends with the sound [n], and the second syllable
begins with the sound [j]. In Italian (and French), both the [n]
and the [j] are sounded at the beginning of the second syllable.
Thus a different symbol [ɲ] is used.
**bá-gno**     [ba ɲɔ]          **só-gno**     [so ɲɔ]          **lé-gno** [le ɲɔ]
**co-gná-to** [ko ɲa tɔ]     **a-gnel-lí-no** [a ɲel:li nɔ]

[ŋ]     occurs when **n** is followed by the sounds [k] or [g] (hard **c** and
hard **g**). It occurs in English in words like **anchor, thank, finger,
hunger,** etc.

**án-che**  [aŋ kɛ]          **an-có-ra** [aŋ ko ra]
**fán-go**  [faŋ gɔ]          **vèn-go**   [vɛŋ gɔ]
**bián-ca** [bjaŋ ka]          **sán-gue**  [saŋ gwɛ]

If you are told that "your Italian does not sound very Italian", consult the following check-list of errors frequently made by American singers. One or more of your faults is probably listed.

1 *Are you pronouncing* [t] *and* [d] *on the teeth?* Use of alveolar instead of dental [t] and [d] is the most conspicuous error made by English-speaking (and German-speaking) singers in Italian. There are famous non-Italian singers who seem to have mastered all the other problems of the language, whose Italian still "does not sound very Italian" just because of this fault.

2 *Are you sliding in and out of vowels?* Italian vowels have the same sound from beginning to end. Form a vowel simultaneously with the consonant preceding it. That will eliminate the sliding in. Do not anticipate formation of an oncoming consonant. That will avoid a sliding out. If there is a diphthong in an Italian word ([ɑ:i], [ɑ:u], etc.), do not anticipate formation of the second vowel.

3 *Are you distinguishing between double and single consonants where written?* Non-Italians can make hilarious mistakes in meaning. The word-rhythm produced by the play of double and single consonants will enhance and complement the musical rhythm. Sometimes it will form a counterpoint to it. All this is very "Italian" and is an extremely important element of the flavor of the language.

4 *Are you using* [I] *and* [U] *instead of* [i] *and* [u] *when these sounds occur before consonants?* Are you allowing a final unstressed **a** (as in **sala**) to sound as [ə] or [ʌ]? These three vowel errors are often made by American singers. The vowels [I], [U], [ə] and [ʌ] do not exist in Italian.

5   *Are your* [e] *and* [o] *too high and round?*  Are they high and round
enough?  Sometimes American singers carry the high sounds of
German and French into Italian. Remember that the Italian closed [e]
and [o] are more relaxed than their French or German counterparts.

On the other hand, [e] and [o] should not be so low that they are
indistinguishable from [ɛ] and [ɔ]. Even Italian singers are sometimes guilty of this error. Faulty reasoning lies behind the excuse
that "opening the vowel makes a more beautiful tone". If that were
true, why not sing everything on **ah** and have done with it?  A
beautiful tone can be achieved on [e] and [o] (Italians have been
doing it for centuries) if you learn how to do it. And in so doing, you
have preserved in your diction the grace and elegance so characteristic of well pronounced Italian.

6   *Is your delivery relaxed and smooth?*  Above all, Italian pronunciation must have these qualities. The language is basically *legato*.
The vowels must flow one into another. There are no stops between
words. Accurate and relaxed Italian pronunciation can only help to
improve singing.

# Ecclesiastical Latin

These rules for the pronunciation of ecclesiastical Latin are based on *The Correct Pronunciation of Latin according to Roman Usage.* Rev. Michael de Angelis, C.R.M.  Philadelphia: St. Gregory Guild, Inc. 1937.

VOWELS

Only five vowels occur in liturgical Latin. They are the Italian vowels [ɑ], [ɛ], [i], [ɔ] and [u]. Italian closed **e** and closed **o** are not used.

[ɑ] is spelled
    **a**   **a-men**    **pax**    **ma-la**    **tu-a**    **na-tu-ra**

Final unstressed **a** should not degenerate into [ə].

[ɛ] is spelled
    **e**   **re-qui-em ae-ter-nam**    **se-dit**
   **ae**   **al-mae**   **quae-cum-quae**    **sae-cu-la sae-cu-lo-rum**
   **oe**   **moe-re-bat**   **coe-lum**

Exception   When the second of two vowels has a dieresis (¨) they are sounded separately.  **Raphaël** [rɑ fɑ ɛl]

[i] spelled
    **i**   is the vowel sound in English **meet**.
    **y**   **in**    **Pa-tri**   **Fi-li-o**   **Spi-ri-tu-i**
       **no-bis**   **fac-ti**   **Ky-ri-e**   **coe-le-stis**

[I] as in English **mitt** is never used.

When two [i] vowels occur in succession, the second must be sounded without a glottal stop.  **filii** [fi li i]

[ɔ] is spelled
   o

The open **o** sound is always used for **o**, but not in **oe**.

| | | |
|---|---|---|
| **Do-mi-ne** | **quo-ni-am** | **no-bis** |
| **mor-tu-os** | **vo-lun-ta-tis** | **vin-cu-lo** |
| **in quo to-tum con-ti-ne-tur** | | |

[u] is spelled
   u

The sound [u] (as in English **moon**) is always used for **u**.

| | | | |
|---|---|---|---|
| **u-num** | **fac-tum** | **Do-mi-num** | **fi-li-us** |
| **lu-men de lu-mi-ne** | | **in-car-na-tus** | |
| **et cum spi-ri-tu tu-o** | | **se-pul-tus** | |

The sound [U] (as in English **foot** or **sure**) is never used.

When a word ends in a vowel and the next word begins with the same vowel, the sound must be reiterated. There should be no separation between the vowel sounds, however, as would be made by a glottal stop.

**Justi in**       [ju sti in]
**Domine exaudi** [dɔ mi nɛ ɛg zɑ u di]
**Lauda anima**    [lɑ u dɑ ɑ ni mɑ]

## DIPHTHONGS

The nine diphthongs of liturgical Latin are pronounced exactly as they look. (Remember that **ae** and **oe** are pronounced [ɛ].) Both vowels must sound clearly, although they may be set to one note. The second vowel of each pair is a little weaker than the first, but it does not have the glide-off effect of English or Italian.

| | | | | | |
|---|---|---|---|---|---|
| ai, ay | **Laicus** | [lɑ i kus] | **Raymundi** | [rɑ i mun di] |
| ou | **coutuntur** | [kɔ u tun tur] | **prout** | [prɔ ut] |
| au | **laudamus** | [lɑ u dɑ mus] | **exaudi** | [ɛg zɑ u di] |
| eu | **euntes** | [ɛ un tɛs] | | |
| ei | **mei** | [mɛ i] | **Deitas** | [dɛ i tɑs] |
| ua | **tua** | [tu ɑ] | | |
| ui | **tui** | [tu i] | | |
| uae | **tuae** | [tuɛ] | | |
| uo | **tuo** | [tu ɔ] | | |

GLIDES

There are two glides in liturgical Latin.

[w]  occurs when **ua, ue, ui** and **uo** are preceded by **q** or **ng**.
**qui**  [kwi]  **quam**  [kwɑm]  **lo-que-bar**  [lɔ kwɛ bɑr]
**quod**  [kwɔd]  **san-guis** [sɑŋ gwis]  **quo-ni-am**  [kwɔ ni ɑm]

This glide is not executed as quickly as in Italian (or English), but rather like a weak [u] vowel preceding a strong, stressed vowel.

Exception  **cui** [ku i] does not have a glide.

[j]  is used when **j** appears. It sounds as in Italian.
**Je-sus**    **e-jus**    **ju-di-ci-um**    **ju-stum**    **Je-ru-sa-lem**

## CONSONANTS

Consonants in Latin should be modeled on Italian rather than English. They are uncomplicated.

When doubled they should be prolonged somewhat (as in Italian).
**ter-ram**        **al-tis-si-mus**        **il-la**        **pec-ca-ta**

Eleven of the consonants are easily pronounced.

**b**, **f**, **m**, **n**, **q** and **v**    are treated as in Italian or English.

**d** and **l**    are treated as in Italian. They are dental—that is, they are formed with the tip of the tongue on the back of the upper teeth. The tongue is completely relaxed.

**p**    is dry, as in Italian.
There is no intrusion of air between the consonant and the vowel that follows it.

**k**    sounds as in English

**r**    receives the same treatment as in Italian.

Flip for a single **r**, trill for double **r**.
Possibly trill on initial **r** for emphasis.

In religious texts the trilled **r** should be used sparingly.

*159 Latin*

*Consonants*
**c, g, gn**

The soft and hard sounds are the same as in Italian.

soft **c, g**  when followed by **e, i, y, ae** and **oe**. [tʃ] [dʒ]

| | | | |
|---|---|---|---|
| **ce-dat** | **ec-ce** | **coe-li** | **cae-li** |
| **suf-fi-cit** | **coe-nae** | | |
| **pan-ge** | **le-ge** | **re-gi-na** | **pla-gae** |

hard **c, g**  when followed by **a, o, u** or consonants. [k] [g]

| | | | |
|---|---|---|---|
| **vo-ca** | **pec-ca-ta** | **co-ram** | **si-cut** |
| **sanc-tus** | **Chri-ste** | | |
| **sur-gant** | **er-go** | **lin-gua** | **glo-ri-a** |

when final.
**nunc**

**gn**  [ɲ] sounds as in Italian or French (**agnello, agneau**), similar to the **ni** in English **onion**.

| | | | |
|---|---|---|---|
| **a-gnus** | **di-gnum** | **ma-gna** | **ma-gni-fi-cat** |

*Consonants*
**h, s, sc, ss, t, th**

**h**  is silent, as in Italian, except that it is sounded as [k] in the two
**mihi, nihil**  words **mihi** [mi ki] and **nihil** [ni kil].

**s**  always receives the unvoiced sound [s].

The sound [z] is not used.

**ss**  is prolonged. [s:s]
| | | | |
|---|---|---|---|
| **sa-lu-ta-re** | **mi-se-re-re** | **o-re-mus** | |
| **cau-sa** | **Je-sum** | **re-sur-rex-it** | **mi-ser** |
| **pas-sus** | **al-tis-si-mus** | | |

**sc**  is treated as in Italian.

**hard sc**  is pronounced [sk] before **a, o, u** and consonants.
| | | | |
|---|---|---|---|
| **re-qui-e-scat** | **vo-bi-scum** | **in-ge-mi-sco** | **scho-la** |

**soft sc**  is pronounced [ʃ] before **e** and **i**.
| | | |
|---|---|---|
| **a-scen-dit** | **re-qui-e-scit** | **vi-sce-ra** |
| **su-sci-pe** | **flo-re-scit** | |

**t**  is pronounced as in Italian—with the tip of the tongue against the
back of the upper teeth. English **t** sounds especially ugly in Latin.
| | | | |
|---|---|---|---|
| **ti-bi** | **tu-a** | **tu-o** | **i-te** | **tol-lis** |
| **ae-ter-nam** | **ti-me-bit** | **et cum spi-ri-tu tu-o** | |

**ti**  followed by a vowel and preceded by any letter except **s, t** or **x**
is pronounced [ts].
| | | |
|---|---|---|
| **gra-ti-as** | [grɑ tsi ɑs] | **pre-ti-o-si** [prɛ tsi ɔ si] |
| **e-ti-am** | [ɛ tsi ɑm] | **ul-ti-o-nis** [ul tsi ɔ nis] |
| **sci-en-ti-am** | [ʃi ɛn tsi ɑm] | **jus-ti-ti-a** [jus ti tsi ɑ] |
| **ten-ta-ti-o-nem** | [tɛn tɑ tsi ɔ nɛm] | |

**th**  is pronounced [t].
**ca-tho-li-cam** [kɑ tɔ li kɑm]

*161 Latin*

x  may be voiced [gz] or unvoiced [ks].

It is voiced when the prefix **ex** begins a word and is followed by a vowel or **h**.

**ex-al-to**  [ɛg zɑl tɔ]      **ex-hi-be-o**  [ɛg zi bɛ ɔ]
**ex-a-u-di** [ɛg zɑ u di]     **ex-a-mi-ne** [ɛg zɑ mi nɛ]

It is unvoiced in all other positions.
**cru-ci-fix-us**    **lux**       **pax**           **dix-it**
**aux-i-li-um**     **ex-su-les** [ɛk su lɛs]   **ex-si-li-um** [ɛk si li um]

When the prefix **ex** is followed by soft **c**, the group is pronounced [ɛkʃ].
**ex-cel-sis** [ɛk ʃɛl sis]      **ex-ces-sus** [ɛk ʃɛs:sus]

z  is sounded [dz].
**La-za-rus** [lɑ dzɑ rus]

Attention is drawn in the following texts to those vowels and consonants often mispronounced according to Roman usage. The correct phonetic symbols are given below.

**Gloria**

Glo—ri—a in ex—cel—sis De—o. Et in ter—ra pax ħo—mi—ni—bus
ɔ     i     εk ʃ   i   ε ɔ    i   r:r        ɔ         u

bo—nae vo—lun—ta—tis. La—u—da—mus te. Be—ne—di—ci—mus te.
ɔ  ε  ɔ u    i          u   ε    ε  ε  tʃ  u    ε

A—do—ra—mus te. Glo—ri—fi—ca—mus te. Gra—ti—as a—gi—mus
ɔ    u    ε          u    ε    ts     dʒ  u

ti—bi prop—ter ma—gnam glo—ri—am tu—am. Do—mi—ne De—us.
ɔ         ɲ                      ɔ     ε  ε u

Rex coe—le—stis, De—us Pa—ter om—ni—po—tens. Do—mi—ne
tʃε  ε  i    ε u         ɔ   s  ɔ       ε

Fi—li u—ni—ge—ni—te, Je—su Chri—ste. Do—mi—ne De—us,
dʒε   ε  εs    i  ε   ɔ     ε  ε u

A—gnus De—i, Fi—li—us Pa—tris. Qui tol—lis pec—ca—ta mun—di:
ɲ u   ε      u      i     ɔl:li   k:k      u

mi—se—re—re no—bis. Qui tol—lis pec—ca—ta mun—di, su—sci—pe
sε  ε  ε ɔ  i      ɔl:li   k:k     u     ʃ    ε

de—pre—ca—ti—o—nem no—stram. Qui se—des ad dex—te—ram
ε  ε    ts ɔ     ɔ         ε         ε

Pa—tris, mi—se—re—re no—bis. Quo—ni—am tu so—lus sanc—tus.
i     sε  ε  ε ɔ  i   ɔ       ɔ u     u

Tu so—lus Do—mi—nus. Tu so—lus al—tis—si—mus Je—su Chri—ste.
ɔ  u  ɔ     u    ɔ  u    s:s    u  εs    i

Cum Sanc—to Spi—ri—tu in glo—ri—a De—i Pa—tris. A—men.
u      ɔ   i       i       ε    i      ε

*Sample Latin text*

**Salve Regina**  Sal—ve, Re—gi—na, ma—ter mi—se—ri—cor—di—ae: Vi—ta,
　　　　　　　　ɛ　　ɛ dʒ　　　　　　　s　　　　　　ɛ

dul—ce—do, et spes no—stra, sal—ve. Ad te cla—ma—mus,
u　tʃ　ɔ　　ɛ　　ɔ　　　　ɛ　　　ɛ　　　　　　u

ex—su—les, fi—li—i He—vae. At te su—spi—ra—mus, ge—men—tes
ɛk su　　　　　ɛ　ɛ　　ɛ　　　　　　u　dʒɛ ɛ　　ɛ

et flen—tes in hac la—cri—ma—rum val—le. E—i—a er—go,
　ɛ　ɛ　　　　u　　l:lɛ ɛ　　　　　ɔ

Ad—vo—ca—ta no—stra, il—los tu—os mi—se—ri—cor—des o—cu—los
　ɔ　　　ɔ　　　il : lɔ　ɔ　　s　　　　　ɔ　　ɔ

ad nos con—ver—te. Et Je—sum, be—ne—dic—tum fruc—tum
　ɔ　ɔ　　　ɛ　　　ɛ su　ɛ　ɛ　i　　u　　u

ven—tris tu—i, no—bis post hoc ex—si—li—um o—sten—de. O
ɛ　i　　　ɔ　i　ɔ　ɔ ɛk si　u　ɔ　　　ɛ ɔ

cle—mens: O pi—a: O dul—cis Vir—go Ma—ri—a.
ɛ　　s ɔ　　　ɔ　u tʃi　i　ɔ

French

This section is intended as a guide to the singing pronunciation of French. There are marked differences between conversational pronunciation (*la diction courante*) and stage diction (*la diction soutenue*, or *le style soutenu*). The rules are based on grammatical and linguistic sources and on the usage of the French stage.

| | |
|---|---|
| [a] | **a, à** la, là  175 |
| [ɑ] | **a, â** pas, âme  176 **33 45** |
| [ɑ̃] | **aen, aën** St. Saëns  189 |
| [ə] or [ɛ] | **ai** (interior) faisons; chaine  178 180 183 **49** |
| [ɛ] or [e] | **ai** (final) vrai, balai; gai, irai  180 182-183 |
| [ɛ] | **aient** parlaient  179 181 183 |
| [aj] | **ail** (within the same syllable) corail  195 **54** |
| [ɛ̃] | **aim, ain** faim, pain  190 **49 50** |
| [ɑ̃] | **am, an** champ, enfant  189 **45 46 47 48** |
| [ɑ̃] | **aon** paon  189 |
| [u] | **aou** saoul  199 210 |
| [o] | **au** faut  184 **26 27 36 51** |
| [ɔ] | **au + r** Fauré  184 |
| [ɛj] | **ay** (je) paye, crayon  181 183 |
| [ɛji] | **ays** pays  210 |
| | |
| mute or [b] | **b** plomb; beau, abord  198 203 |
| [p] | **b** absolu  203 |
| silent | **b** (final) plomb  198 |
| | |
| silent or [k] | **c** (final) jonc; lac  198 |
| [k] | **c + a, o, u** cave, coeur, curé  205 **71 72** |
| [s] | **c + e, i, y** cette, cil, cygne  207 |
| [k] | **c + consonant** cri, crayon  205 |
| [s] | **ç** leçon  207 |
| [k] or [ks] | **cc** accident; accabler  208 |
| [ʃ] | **ch** chat, marcher  205 **74** |
| [k] | **ch** choeur, écho  205 |
| | |
| [d] | **d** dent, dieu, dure  204 **69** |
| silent | **d** (final) nid  199 **69** |
| | |
| [ə] or [ɛ] | **e** je, cheval; des, bref  178 180-181 183 **23 49** |
| [ɛ] | **è, ê** lèvre, tête  180 183 **23** |
| [e] | **é** parlé  182 183 **17 18** |
| [ɑ̃] | **ean** vengeance  189 |
| [o] | **eau** beau  184 **26 27 36 51** |
| [e] or [ɛf] | **ef** (final) clef; bref  181-182 199 |
| [ɛ] | **ei** neige  181 **23** |
| [ɛj] | **eil** soleil  181 195 **55** |
| [ɛ̃] | **eim, ein** Reims, sein  190 **49 50** |
| [ɑ̃] | **em, en** embaumer  189 **45 46 47 48** |
| [amɑ̃] | **emment** (adverb) ardemment  191 |
| [ɑ̃] | **en** enfant  189 **45 46 47 48** |
| [jɛ̃] | **en** (preceded by **i** or **y**) bien, moyen  189 190 **49** |
| [ə] or [ɑ̃] | **ent** parlent (verb), souvent  178 189 |
| [e] or [ɛr] | **er** (final) parler, léger; fer  182 200 |
| [y] | **eu, eû** (j'ai) eu, (qu'il) eût  187 |

| | |
|---|---|
| [ø] or [œ] | **eu** peu, berceuse; peur 186 **36 37 42 43 44** |
| [œj] | **euil** deuil 186 **56** |
| [œ̃] | **eun** jeun 190 **53** |
| [ɛks] or [ɛgz] | **ex** extase; exhaler 208 |
| [e] | **ez** (final) nez, assez 182 202 **17 18** |
| | |
| silent or [f] | **f** clef; faut, chef 199 204 **73** |
| | |
| [g] | **g** + **a**, **o**, **u** gare 205 **72** |
| [g] | **g** + consonant grand 205 |
| [ʒ] | **g** + **e**, **i**, **y** geler, givre, gymnopédie 205 **74** |
| silent | **g** (final) rang 199 |
| [ɲ] | **gn** agneau 206 **65** |
| [g] | **gu** guerre, guide 205 **72** |
| [gɥ] | **gu** aiguille 205 |
| | |
| silent | **h** haut 209 |
| | |
| [i] | **i**, **î** ici 177 **15 17 35** |
| [j] | **i** + vowel tiens 195 **61** |
| [je] | **ied** pied 182 **61** |
| [jɛ̃] or [jɑ̃] | **ien** bien; patience 189 190 **49** |
| [je] or [jɛr] | **ier** premier; hier, fier 182 200 |
| [j] | **il** corail 195 **54** |
| silent or [il] | **il** (final) fusil; il, avril 199 |
| [il] | **il** or **ill** (initial) illusion 177 195 |
| [ijə] | **ille** (final) famille 195 |
| [ilə] | **ille** (final) mille, ville, tranquille 195 |
| [ɛ̃] | **im**, **in** timbre, fin 190 **49 50** |
| [jɔ̃] | **ion** occasion 190 |
| | |
| [ʒ] | **j** je, jurer 205 **74** |
| | |
| [k] | **k** kilomètre 205 |
| | |
| [l] | **l**, **ll** loin, aller, folle 206 **78** |
| silent or [l] | **l** (final) fusil; seul, avril 199 **78** |
| [j] | **ll** (after **i**) billet, piller 195 |
| | |
| [m] | **m** mère 206 |
| [n] | **mn** damner, automne 206 |
| | |
| [n] | **n** nuit 206 |
| | |
| [o] or [ɔ] | **o** pot, rose; porte 184 **26 27 36 51** |
| [o] | **ô** côté, trône 184 **26 27 36 51** |
| [œj] | **oeil** oeil 186 **56** |
| [ø] or [œ] | **oeu** voeu; coeur 186 **36 37 44** |
| [wa] | **oi** voix, fois 175 194 **62** |

| | | |
|---|---|---|
| [wɛ̃] | **oin** | coin, point 190 **49 50** |
| [õ] | **om, on** | ombre, fond 190 **51 52** |
| [õ] | **ompt** (final) | prompt, rompt 190 203 |
| [u] | **ou, où, oû** | fou, oû, goûter 177 **24 25 27** |
| [w] | **ou** + vowel | oui, fouet 194 **62** |
| [waj] | **oy** | voyons 194 |

| | | |
|---|---|---|
| [p] | **p** | papa, père 203 **67** |
| silent | **p** | baptême 203 |
| silent | **p** (final) | drap, champ 199 |
| [f] | **ph** | phare 204 |
| [pt] or [t] | **pt** | somptueux; sculpteur 203 |

| | | |
|---|---|---|
| [k] | **q** (final) | coq 199 |
| [k] | **qu** | quatre, qui 205 **71 72** |

| | | |
|---|---|---|
| [r] | **r** | rameau, sortez 206 **80** |
| silent or [r] | **r** (final) | premier; partir 200 **80** |

| | | |
|---|---|---|
| [s] | **s** (initial, interior) | sortir, jasmin, aspect 207 |
| [z] | **s** (intervocalic) | rosier, choisir 208 |
| silent or [s] | **s** (final) | repos, sors; lys, jadis 201 |
| [sk] | **sc** + **a, o, u** or consonant | scandale, esclave, sculpteur 207 |
| [s] | **sc** + **e, i, y** | scie, science 207 |
| [s] | **ss** | passer 207 |

| | | |
|---|---|---|
| silent or [t] | **t** | tôt, nuit; tête, futile 202 204 **69 70** |
| [sj] | **ti** | nation, patient 207 |

| | | |
|---|---|---|
| [y] | **u, û** | dure, fût 187 **35** |
| [ɥ] | **u** + vowel | nuit, nuage 187 193 **63** |
| [œj] | **ueil** | cueillir, accueil 186 **56** |
| [œ̃] | **um, un** | parfum, brun 190 **53** |
| [ɥij] | **uy** | fuyez 193 |

| | | |
|---|---|---|
| [v] | **v** | vivre 204 **73** |

| | | |
|---|---|---|
| [v] | **w** | wagon 204 |

| | | |
|---|---|---|
| [ks] or [gz] | **x** | extase, exister 208 |
| [s] or [z] | **x** | soixante; sixième 208 |
| silent | **x** (final) | faux 202 |

| | | |
|---|---|---|
| [i] | **y** | cygne 177 **17** |
| [j] | **y** + vowel | yeux, foyer 195 **61** |
| [jɛ̃] | **yen** | moyen 190 |
| [ɛ̃] | **ym, yn** | thym, syncope 190 **50** |

| | | |
|---|---|---|
| silent or [z] | **z** | allez, zèle 202 208 |

*169 French*

**Dubois, Marguérite-Marie**   1960   Larousse dictionnaire moderne. Paris: Librairie Larousse (French-English)

**Warnant, Leon**   1968   Dictionnaire de la pronunciation française. Gembloux: Editions J. Duculot.

The Larousse dictionary, and most other French dictionaries, indicate pronunciation for conversational French. Their usefulness for the singer is mainly for translation.

The Warnant dictionary is a pronouncing dictionary, containing no definitions. It is of great value to the singer, however, for it indicates both styles of pronunciation where there is a divergence: conversational, abbreviated *cour.* and stage diction, abbreviated *sout.* The third edition, published in 1968, contains 235 pages of listings of personal and place names.

**Fouché, Pierre**   1959   Traité de la prononciation française. Paris: Librairie Klincksieck (In French; very complete and extremely well organized.)

**Bernac, Pierre**   1970   The Interpretation of French Song. New York: Praeger Publishers

Other references are listed in the Bibliography.

*Syllabification*

In dividing French words into syllables:

1   A single consonant between two vowels goes with the second.
    **a-mi-tié**          **pré-si-dent**

    except for **x**.
    **ex-is-ter**

2   Consonants followed by **l** or **r** and the combinations **ch, gn, ph,**
    and **th** go with the following vowel.
    **é-clos**            **mai-gre**          **mou-choir**
    **a-gneau**           **pro-phè-te**       **go-thi-que**

    But when **r** and **l** occur in succession, they divide between syllables.
    **par-ler**           **hor-lo-ge**

3   Otherwise, consonants (including double consonants) divide
    between syllables.
    **al-bâ-tre**         **om-bre**           **mon-de**
    **par-tez**           **des-cends**        **ex-ta-se**
    **ob-jet**            **sep-tem-bre**      **mal-gré**
    **om-bra-ge**         **mar-bre**          **es-clave**
    **don-ner**           **oc-cu-per**

Occasionally in French, a word contains a vowel surmounted by two dots. This is not an umlaut, as in German, but a dieresis, as in English (**naïve** or **coöperate**). Ordinarily, a syllable in the interior of a French word begins with a consonant or a glide. The dieresis indicates that the vowel over which it is placed is the beginning of a new syllable. In words like **naïf**, it serves further to indicate that the **ai** do not form a combination (giving [ɛ]) but belong to separate syllables.

| | | |
|---|---|---|
| **haïr** [a ir] | **Noël** [nɔ ɛl] | **païen** [pa jɛ̃] |
| **naïf** [na if] | **aïeux** [a jø] | **naïade** [na ja də] |
| **laïc** [la ik] | **Gaït** [ga it] | **Thaïs** [ta is] |

VOWELS

Chart of French vowels, showing relative height, roundness, opening
and closure.

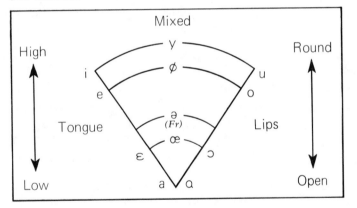

**ah** *vowels*

French has two different **ah** vowels. The more characteristic is the bright [a], produced with slightly more of a smile than the Italianate [ɑ].

In modern conversational French, differentiation between these vowels has all but disappeared. The [a] is used almost exclusively. The stage language, however, is more conservative, and authorities insist on a difference.

When differentiating between the vowels in singing, Americans must consider the following points:

1  The difference between the two **ah** vowels is very slight; it should not be exaggerated.

2  American singers, especially the inexperienced, tend to sing [ɑ] too darkly. There is a danger of darkening [ɑ] too much when differentiating it from [a].

3  The [a] should not be widened (spread) to the point where it begins to sound like [æ], the vowel in English **cat**. [a] is a good [ɑ], pronounced with more smile to get a brighter sound.

What these points stress is that the differentiation is a subtle one and will be most obvious when the two vowels occur in close succession, as in **là-bas** [la bɑ]. The American singer should first establish a good [a]; this is by far the more frequent and is very characteristic of French. It would not be at all harmful for the student to use [a] exclusively for a short period of time. The refinement of [ɑ] can be re-introduced after [a] has been established in the voice.

**ah** *vowels*
    [a]

[a] is used

1    for the spelling **à**, and most of the time for the spelling **a**.
    **là**    **la**    **baba**

but not when the **a** is used in combination with other vowels.
**aimer** [ɛ me]    **jaune** [ʒo nə]

and not when **a** is followed by an **m** or **n** in the same syllable, unless that **m** or **n** is part of a double consonant.
**année** [a]    **Grammont** [a]    (but not **l'an** or **champ**)

2    in the combination sound [wa] for the spelling **oi**.
    **toi**    **noir**

but not for **trois** [trwɑ]

3    the combination sound [waj] for the spelling **oy**.
    **voyez**    **royal**

Examples of words using [a]:

| | | | | |
|---|---|---|---|---|
| capable | car | cravate | chat | dada |
| dame | drapeau | fané | fade | fracas |
| gala | garder | grenat | habit | jamais |
| jardin | jasmin | lac | lame | larme |
| latin | ma | mal | marbre | mardi |
| nabab | nappe | nature | papa | par |
| parole | rabat | race | ramier | table |
| tracas | va | val | vache | Voilà la salade! |

| | | | | |
|---|---|---|---|---|
| choix | doigt | doit | foi | fois |
| angoisse | joie | loi | loisir | émoi |
| moi | noir | poire | poison | roi |
| soi | soif | soir | toi | toit |
| voie | voile | voir | voisin | voiture |
| foyer | joyau | joyeux | loyal | noyez |
| royal | voyage | voyante | doyen | moyen |

**ah** *vowels*
  [ɑ]

[ɑ] is used

1  for **â**.
   **âme**    **pâle**    **mâle**    **câlin**

2  in names of musical syllables.
   **fa**      **la**

3  for **a** followed by unvoiced **s**.
   **hélas**    **passer**

Exceptions  **chasse, débarasse, masse, paillasse,** and all verbs in **-asse, -asses, -assent.**

4  for **a** followed by voiced **s**.
   **extase**    **occasion**    **gaz**

5  for **a** followed by silent **s**.
   **pas**      **bas**      **las**      **trépas**

Exception  All verbs ending in **-as**.

6  in a number of other words, among which, most commonly occurring
   in musical texts are:
   **accabler** [a kɑ ble]      **bataille** [ba tɑ jə]      **cadavre** [ka dɑ vrə]
   **gars** [gɑ]

| | | | | |
|---|---|---|---|---|
| Anne | bramer | chocolate | clamer | climat |
| condamner | crabe | damner | déclamer | diable |
| diffamer | enflammer | enlacer | érafler | esclave |
| espace | fable | flamme | funérailles | gagner |
| gare | grave | havre | jable | Jeanne |
| lacer | miracle | navrer | oracle | paille |
| prélat | proclamer | racler | railler | rare |
| réclamer | sable | | | |

7  for **trois** [trwɑ].

*176 French*

*Vowels*
[i] [u]

[i] is spelled

| i | il | tire | vive | ici | fine |
|---|---|---|---|---|---|
| î | île | dîner | | | |
| y | lyre | martyr | style | cyprès | hymne | anonyme |

[i] is used  when **i** is followed by a double **n** or **m**.

**innocent**          **innombrable**          **immense**

[i] is not used  if the **i** or **y** is followed by a single **n** or **m** occurring in the same syllable.

Note that the sound [I], as in English **fit**, is never used in French.

[u] is spelled

| ou | ou | doux | fou | loup |
|---|---|---|---|---|
| | filou | courir | mourir | amour |
| | court | jour | lourd | tournez |
| oû | coûte | goûte | | |
| où | où | | | |

Note that the sound [U], as in the English **foot**, is never used in French. The French vowel [u] is similar to the vowel in English **moon** but is pronounced with the lips in a more puckered position.

*Vowels*
[ə]

The sound of the French neutral vowel [ə] has no approximation in English.

| | | | | | |
|---|---|---|---|---|---|
| **je** | [ʒə] | **cheval** | [ʃə val] | **chemise** | [ʃə mi zə] |
| **premier** | [prə mje] | **leçon** | [lə sõ] | **velours** | [və lur] |
| **élever** | [e lə ve] | **revenir** | [rə və nir] | **parlerez** | [par lə re] |
| **fenêtre** | [fə nɛ trə] | **venez** | [və ne] | **apercevrez** | [a pɛr sə vre] |
| **cloches** | [klɔ ʃə] | **livres** | [li vrə] | **lampes** | [lã pə] |
| **fumes** | [fy mə] | **gardes** | [gar də] | **ouvres** | [u vrə] |
| **furent** | [fy rə] | **donnèrent** | [dɔ nɛ rə] | **pressent** | [prɛ sə] |

[ə] is sounded

1     when the **e** has no accent mark and ends a syllable.
     **je**      **cheval**      **fenêtre**

     Note: A plural noun or adjective ending in **-es** is also pronounced [ə]. Singular and plural sound alike.

| | | | |
|---|---|---|---|
| **fenêtre** | [fə nɛ trə] | **fenêtres** | [fə nɛ trə] |
| **lettre** | [lɛ trə] | **lettres** | [lɛ trə] |
| **belle** | [bɛ lə] | **belles** | [bɛ lə] |

2     for the ending **-es** of second person singular in verbs.
     **tu parles** [parlə]      **donnes** [dɔ nə]

3     for the ending **-ent** of third person plural in verbs.
     **ils parlent** [parlə]      **donnent** [dɔ nə]

4     for some forms of the verb **faire** (notably those forms in which **ai** is followed by the sound [z]).

| | | | | | |
|---|---|---|---|---|---|
| **faisons** | [fə zõ] | **faisant** | [fə zã] | **faisais** | [fə zɛ] |
| **faisait** | [fə zɛ] | **faisiez** | [fə zje] | **faisions** | [fə zjõ] |

[ə] is silent

1   when a word ending in [ə] is elided to a word beginning with a vowel.
    **autre amour** [o tra mur]    **penche aussi** [pã ʃo si]

2   in the third person plural ending of the imperfect tense.
    **parlaient** [par lɛ]   *not*   [par lɛə]

3   in the interior of a word when it is preceded by another vowel.
    **gaiement** [ge mã]    **dévouement** [de vu mã]

4   It is often advisable to omit [ə] after the sound [ø]:
    **queue** [kø]   *not*   [køə]
    **bleues** [blø]   *not*   [bløə]

    and after the sound [wa]:
    **soie** [swa]   *not*   [swaə]
    **joie** [ʒwa]   *not*   [ʒwaə]

[ɛ] is used

1  in **les**, **mes**, **tes**, **ses**, **ces**, **des**, **est**, **es**  [lɛ] etc.

    In conversational French, these words are often pronounced with closed **e**, but in singing, the **e** must always be opened.

2  for **ai** when it is followed by anything in the same word.

| | | | | | | |
|---|---|---|---|---|---|---|
| **fais** | [fɛ] | **paix** | [pɛ] | **air** | [ɛr] | **jamais** [ʒa mɛ] |
| **parlerais** | [par lə rɛ] | **haie** | [ɛ] | **irais** | [i rɛ] | |
| **plaisir** | [plɛ zir] | **parlaient** | [par lɛ] | **aimer** | [ɛ me] | |

Exception  When **ai** is followed by a single **l**, **m** or **n** in the same syllable. (See pages 178, 190, 195.)

3  for the ending **-ai** in nouns.
    **balai** [ba lɛ]   **essai** [ɛ sɛ]   **mai** [mɛ]   **délai** [de lɛ]

4  for the adjectives **vrai** and **bai**.  [vrɛ], [bɛ]

5  for **è**    **grève** [grɛ və]   **père** [pɛ rə]

6  for **ê**    **tête** [tɛ tə]   **être** [ɛ trə]

7 for **ei** when it is not followed by **m** or **n** in the same syllable.
**neige** [nɛ ʒə] **seine** [sɛ nə]

8 when **e** is followed by a consonant (silent or sounded) in the same syllable. (Except for the endings listed on page 182 under [e])

| | | |
|---|---|---|
| **bref** [brɛf] | **cadet** [ka dɛ] | **spectre** [spɛk trə] |
| **sept** [sɛt] | **vert** [vɛr] | **esclave** [ɛ sklɑ və] |
| **met** [mɛ] | **sec** [sɛk] | **bouquet** [bu kɛ] |
| **mer** [mɛr] | **objet** [ɔb ʒɛ] | **descends** [dɛ sɑ̃] |
| **cher** [ʃɛr] | **aspect** [a spɛ] | **espace** [ɛ spɑ sə] |

9 **eil** produces [ɛj].
**soleil** [sɔ lɛj] **sommeil** [sɔ mɛj] **veiller** [vɛ je] **abeille** [a bɛ jə]

10 **ay** produces [ɛj].
**payer** [pɛ je] **crayon** [krɛ jõ] **rayon** [rɛ jõ]

11 **-aient** (third person plural of verbs in the imperfect tense) is pronounced [ɛ].
**parlaient** [par lɛ]

*Vowels*
[e]

[e] is used

1 for **é**.
**été** [e te]   **allé** [a le]
**fané** [fa ne]   **vérité** [ve ri te]   **espéré** [ε spe re]

2 in the infinitive ending **-er**.
**aller** [a le]   **lever** [lə ve]
**parler** [par le]   **donner** [dɔ ne]   **aimer** [ε me]

3 for nouns and adjectives ending in:
-ier   **pommier** [pɔ mje]   **premier** [prə mje]
-yer   **foyer** [fwa je]   **loyer** [lwa je]
-cher   **archer** [ar ʃe]   **rocher** [rɔ ʃe]
-ger   **berger** [bɛr ʒe]   **léger** [le ʒe]
-eiller   **oreiller** [ɔ rɛ je]

Note that in all of these endings the **r** is silent.

Exceptions   **cher** [ʃɛr]   **fier** [fjɛr]   **hier** [jɛr] *or* [i jɛr]

4 in words ending **-ez**.
**allez** [a le]   **chez** [ʃe]   **nez** [ne]

5 in words ending **-ied**.
**pied** [pje]   **s'assied** [sa sje]

6 in the adjective **gai** and its derivatives.
**gai** [ge]   **gaieté** [ge te]   **gaiement** [ge mɑ̃]

7 for the conjunction **et** [e] and the nouns **quai** [ke] and **clef** [kle].

8 for the ending **-ai** in verbs.
**irai** [i re]   **coupai** [ku pe]   **parlerai** [par lə re]   **donnai** [dɔ ne]

When a word begins with capital **é** the accent mark may be omitted.
It must still be pronounced [e]. (**Eglise, Ecoute**, etc.)
*182 French*

*Summary of spelled* **e**

| [ɛ] | [e] | [ə] |
|---|---|---|
| 1 When followed by silent or sounded consonant in the same syllable.<br>**les  bref  esclave** | 1 With acute accent.<br>**été** | 1 Without an accent mark when ending the syllable.<br>**demi** |
| 2 In the combination **ei**.<br>**neige** | 2 Verbs in **-er**.<br>**parler** | 2 For verbs in **-ent**.<br>**parlent** |
| 3 With grave or circumflex accents.<br>**père  tête** | 3 Words in  **-ier**<br>             **-yer**<br>             **-cher**<br>             **-ger**<br>             **-eiller**<br>             **-ied**<br>             **-ez** | 3 For nouns, adjectives and verbs in **-es**.<br>**lettres**<br>**belles**<br>**donnes** |
| 4 When followed by **il**.<br>**soleil** | 4 For **et, clef** | |

*Summary of spelled* **ai, ay**

| Initial and interior **ai** | Final **ai** | **ay** |
|---|---|---|
| [ɛ] when followed by a vowel or a consonant, silent or sounded (anything but **l**, **m** or **n** in the same syllable). | [ɛ] in all nouns<br>**mai**<br>except **quai** | [ɛj] always |
| [ɛ] in **-aient** | [ɛ] in the adjectives<br>**vrai  bai** | |
| [ə] in **faisons, faisais, faisait, faisant**, etc. | [e] in all verbs<br>**j'ai  je donnai**<br>**je donnerai** | |
| | [e] in the adjective<br>**gai** | |

NB 1. In words like **corail** [kɔ raj], **travail** [tra vaj], **railler** [rɑ je], **travailler** [tra va je], etc., **ai** does not form a combination. It is superseded by the combination **il**. See page 195

NB 2. **ai** followed by a single **m** or **n** in the same syllable is a nasal vowel.

*183 French*

*Vowels*
[o] [ɔ]

[o] is used

1    when the **o** has a circumflex accent.
     **drôle    côté    nôtre    vôtre    arôme    trône**

Exceptions    **hôtel    hôpital**

2    when the **o** is followed by a silent final consonant.
     **mot    idiot    Gounod    oh    dos    repos    gros**

3    when the **o** is followed by the voiced **s** sound.
     **rose** [ro zə]    **poser** [po ze]    **arroser** [a ro ze]
     **oser** [o ze]    **chose** [ʃo zə]    **Berlioz** [bɛr ljoz]

4    for the spellings **au** and **eau**.
     **autre    jaune    faut    faux    Lescaut    aube**
     **beau    cadeau    eau    marteau    chapeau    Beaune**

Exception    **au** is pronounced [ɔ] when it occurs before **r**.

5    for words ending in **-o**.
     **écho    kilo    o!    zéro    numéro**

[ɔ] is used

1    for **o** in all cases not covered by rules for closed **o**.
     **porte** [pɔr tə]    **donner** [dɔ ne]    **odeur** [ɔ dœr]
     **noble** [nɔ blə]    **colère** [kɔ lɛ rə]    **obéir** [ɔ be ir]
     **joli** [ʒɔ li]    **sommeil** [sɔ mɛj]    **voler** [vɔ le]

2    for **au** when it is followed by **r**.
     **aura** [ɔ ra]    **laurier** [lɔ rje]    **Fauré** [fɔ re]
     **saurai** [sɔ re]    **aurore** [ɔ rɔ rə]    **auréole** [ɔ re ɔ lə]

3    for the adjective **mauvais** [mɔ vɛ].

*Summary of* **o, au, eau**

     **o**   is pronounced open [ɔ] in all cases

except 1   when it has a circumflex accent. **ô drôle**

       2   when it is followed by a silent consonant. **mot**

       3   when it is followed by the sound [z]. **rose**

       4   when it is final. **écho**

   **au**   is pronounced closed [o] unless followed by **r**.
        **faut** [fo]   *but*   **Fauré** [fɔ re]

 **eau**   is always pronounced closed [o]. **beau**

*Vowels*
[ø] [œ]

[ø] and [œ] are closed and open forms of the same vowel. They exist in German in **Höhle** and **Hölle**, but not in English.

[ø] is used

1    when **eu** or **oeu** is final or when it is followed by a silent final consonant. In other words, [ø] is used when it is the last sound in the word.

| | | | |
|---|---|---|---|
| peu [pø] | feu [fø] | bleu [blø] | queue [kø] |
| peut [pø] | deux [dø] | cheveux [ʃə vø] | monsieur [mə sjø] |
| voeu [vø] | noeud [nø] | oeufs [ø] | boeufs [bø] |

2    when **eu** is followed by a voiced **s**.

| | |
|---|---|
| berceuse [bɛr sø zə] | chartreuse [ʃar trø zə] |
| chanteuse [ʃɑ tø zə] | vendeuse [vɑ̃ dø zə] |

3    when **eu** is followed by [t], [k], [d], [ʒ] or [m], but these words occur rarely.

neutre     Polyeucte     leude     Maubeuge     neume

[œ] is used

1    when **eu** or **oeu** is followed by a sounded consonant other than [z].

| | | |
|---|---|---|
| fleur [flœ˙r] | heure [œ rə] | coeur [kœr] |
| boeuf [bœf] | seul [sœl] | épreuve [e prœ və] |
| jeune [ʒœ nə] | peuple [pœ plə] | aveugle [a vœ glə] |
| oeuf [œf] | neuf [nœf] | soeur [sœr] |

2    when **eu** or **oe** is followed by **il** to produce [œj].

| | | |
|---|---|---|
| deuil [dœj] | feuille [fœ jə] | écureuil [e ky rœj] |
| seuil [sœj] | oeil [œj] | oeillet [œ jɛ] |

3    when **ue** is followed by **il**.

| | | |
|---|---|---|
| accueil [a kœj] | cercueil [sɛr kœj] | cueillir [kœ jir] |
| écueil [e kœj] | orgueil [ɔr gœj] | recueil [rə kœj] |

**Heureux**    may be pronounced [œ rø] or [ø rø], the first being the more conservative. Likewise, **heureuse** may be [œ rø zə] or [ø rø zə].

*186 French*

*Vowels*
[y] [ɥ]

[y] exists in German **früh** and **grün** but not in English.

[y] is used
1   for **u** or **û** not in combination with other vowels
(such combinations as are found in **faut**, **feu**, **fou**, etc.)

| | | | |
|---|---|---|---|
| **du** [dy] | **rue** [ry (ə)] | **flûte** [fly tə] | **pointu** [pwɛ̃ ty] |
| **sur** [syr] | **mur** [myr] | **jurer** [ʒy re] | **ceinture** [sɛ̃ ty rə] |
| **cru** [kry] | **plus** [ply] | **jupe** [ʒy pə] | **humaine** [y mɛ nə] |

2   for some parts of the verb **avoir**, notably those spelled with **eu**.
This is the only example of **eu** pronounced [y].

| | | | | |
|---|---|---|---|---|
| **il a eu** [i la y] | **eus** | **eûmes** | **eûtes** | **eurent** |
| **eusse** | **eusses** | **eût** | **eussions** | **eussiez** | **eussent** |

[ɥ] is a glide existing only in French. It is formed in the same way as [y], but the sound is intensified and passes quickly and smoothly to the following vowel.

[ɥ] is used   whenever **u** is followed by a vowel other than the neutral vowel.
**nuit** [nɥi]   **suis** [sɥi]   **puit** [pɥi]   **cuire** [kɥi rə]

The glide [ɥ] must **never** be replaced by the glide [w].

*Nasalization*

Nasalization occurs when a vowel is followed by **m** or **n** in the same syllable.

| | | | |
|---|---|---|---|
| Nasal | **an** | **sein** | **brun** |
| Not Nasal | **â-ne** | **sei-ne** | **bru-ne** |

When **m** or **n** are part of a double consonant (**mm**, **nn** or **mn**) no nasalization occurs.

| | | | | | |
|---|---|---|---|---|---|
| Nasal | **an** | **Jean** | **bon** | **ombre** | |
| Not Nasal | **année** | **Jeanne** | **bonne** | **homme** | **damne** [dɑ nə] |

When a vowel is nasalized, the **m** or **n** following is not sounded, except in elision.

*Nasals*
[ã]

[ã] is spelled

| | | | | | |
|---|---|---|---|---|---|
| an | **tant** | [tã] | **parlant** | [par lã] |
| en | **encore** | [ãkɔ rə] | **enfant** | [ã fã] |
| am | **champ** | [ʃã] | **ambre** | [ã brə] |
| em | **temps** | [tã] | **semble** | [sã blə] |
| ean | **Jean** | [ʒã] | **vengeance** | [vã ʒã sə] |
| aen | **St. Saens** | [sɛ̃ sãs] | **Messiaen** | [me sjã] or [mɛ sjã] |
| aon | **paon** | [pã] | **Laon** | [lã] |

Exceptions

1    Remember that 3rd person plural verbs ending in **-ent** are pronounced [ə].

2    When **en** is preceded by **i** or **y**, it is usually pronounced [jɛ̃], as in **bien** [bjɛ̃]. (see [ɛ̃])

The noun ending **-ience** is pronounced [jã sə], and the adjective ending **-ient** [jã].

| | | | |
|---|---|---|---|
| **patience** | [pa sjã sə] | **patient** | [pa sjã] |
| **conscience** | [kõ sjã sə] | **conscient** | [kõ sjã] |

*Nasals*

[ɛ̃] [õ] [œ̃]

[ɛ̃] is spelled

| | | | | | |
|---|---|---|---|---|---|
| in | **fin** | [fɛ̃] | **chemin** | [ʃə mɛ̃] |
| im | **timbre** | [tɛ̃ brə] | **impossible** | [ɛ̃ pɔ si blə] |
| ein | **plein** | [plɛ̃] | **sein** | [sɛ̃] |
| eim | **Reims** | [rɛ̃s] | | |
| ain | **main** | [mɛ̃] | **sain** | [sɛ̃] |
| aim | **faim** | [fɛ̃] | | |
| yn | **syncope** | [sɛ̃ kɔ pə] | **Jocelyn** | [ʒɔ sə lɛ̃] |
| ym | **thym** | [tɛ̃] | **symphonie** | [sɛ̃ fɔ ni ə] |

| | | | | |
|---|---|---|---|---|
| ien, yen | produce [jɛ̃]. | **bien** [bjɛ̃] | **moyen** [mwa jɛ̃] |
| oin | produces [wɛ̃]. | **coin** [kwɛ̃] | **soin** [swɛ̃] |

[õ] is spelled

| | | | | |
|---|---|---|---|---|
| on | **bon** | [bõ] | **fond** | [fõ] |
| om | **ombre** | [õ brə] | **dompter** | [dõ te] |
| eon | **mangeons** | [mã ʒõ] | **forgeons** | [fɔr ʒõ] |

In French conversation, a more open vowel [ɔ̃] is usually used. In singing, however, the use of [õ], based on the vowel [o], avoids a possible confusion with the sound [ɑ̃].

[œ̃] is spelled

| | | | | |
|---|---|---|---|---|
| un | **commun** | [kɔ mœ̃] | **défunt** | [de fœ̃] |
| um | **parfum** | [par fœ̃] | **humble** | [œ̃ blə] |
| eun | **jeun** | [ʒœ̃] | | |

| | |
|---|---|
| **em**<br>**rem** | Although **mm** and **nn** after a vowel usually indicate no nasalization, in words of French origin, beginning with the prefixes **em** and **rem**, the first syllable is nasalized. |

| | | | |
|---|---|---|---|
| **emmasser** [ɑ̃ma se] | | **emmécher** [ɑ̃me ʃe] | |
| **emmener** [ɑ̃ mə ne] | | **emmêler** [ɑ̃mɛ le] | |
| **emménager** [ɑ̃me na ʒe] | | **emmitoufler** [ɑ̃mi tu fle] | |
| **remmener** [rɑ̃ mə ne] | | | |

| | |
|---|---|
| **en** | is pronounced [ɑ̃] before **n** in words of French origin beginning with the prefix **en**. |

**ennoblir** [ɑ̃ nɔ blir]     **ennuie** [ɑ̃ nɥi ə]
**ennuyer** [ɑ̃ nɥi je]

Special cases   **enivrer** [ɑ̃ ni vre]   **enamourer** [ɑ̃ na mu re]   **ennemi** [ɛ nə mi]

In other cases instead of nasalization the vowel changes its value to [a].

| | |
|---|---|
| **emm** | is pronounced [am] in adverbs ending in **-emment**. |

**prudemment** [pry da mɑ̃]    **ardemment** [ar da mɑ̃]

is pronounced [am] in the noun **femme** [fa mə].

| | |
|---|---|
| **enn** | is pronounced [an] in the adjective **solennel** [sɔ la nɛl]. |

Otherwise:

| | |
|---|---|
| **emm** | is pronounced [ɛm]. |

**flemme** [flɛ mə]   **gemme** [ʒɛ mə]

| | |
|---|---|
| **enn** | is pronounced [ɛn]. |

**ennemi** [ɛ nə mi]   **mienne** [mjɛ nə]

## GLIDES

The three French glides [ɥ], [w] and [j] may be considered shortened and intensified forms of [y], [u] and [i]. These semi-vowels glide smoothly and quickly into a following vowel and are more intense than Italian glides. Because they are semi-vowels they must be clearly voiced.

*Glides*
[ɥ]

[ɥ] is used

1　when **u** is followed by a vowel other than the neutral vowel [ə].
It is an intensified [y], and [w] must never be substituted for it.

| | | | | | |
|---|---|---|---|---|---|
| **suis** [sɥi] | **puis** | [pɥi] | **conduit** | [kõ dɥi] |
| **nuit** [nɥi] | **bruit** | [brɥi] | **luire** | [lɥi rə] |
| **lui** [lɥi] | **depuis** | [də pɥi] | **ennuie** | [ã nɥi ə] |

Exception　No glide: **rue**, **élue**, **crue**, etc. [ry ə] etc.

Note that after **g**, **u** normally does not glide. Its purpose
is to harden the **g**.

| | | |
|---|---|---|
| **languir** [lã gir] | **guette** [gɛ tə] | **Guy** [gi] |

Only in one word does it glide: **aiguille** [ɛ gɥi jə] and its
derivatives **aiguillon**, **aiguiser**, etc.

2　In poetry and in musical settings **u** is often separated syllabically
from the vowel following it. In such cases the **u** is rendered simply
as [y]. Thus, **nuage** could be two syllables **nua-ge** [nɥa ʒə] or
three syllables **nu-a-ge** [ny a ʒə].

| | | | | | | |
|---|---|---|---|---|---|---|
| **tuer** [tɥe] | *or* | [ty e] | **tueur** [tɥœr] | *or* | [ty œr] |
| **lueur** [lɥœr] | *or* | [ly œr] | **sueur** [sɥœr] | *or* | [sy œr] |

3　When **u** is followed by **y** the result is [ɥij].

| | | | |
|---|---|---|---|
| **fuyez** [fɥi je] | | **appuyez** [a pɥi je] |
| **essuyer** [ɛ sɥi je] | | **ennuyez** [ã nɥi je] |

*193 French*

*Glides*
[w]

[w] spelled

**ou**    followed by a vowel (other than the neutral vowel) produces either [w] or [uw] depending on the number of notes allotted to the sound group.

    one note:   **oui**  [wi]      **ouest** [wɛst]    **jouer** [ʒwe]
    two notes: **jou-et** [ʒu wɛ]  **rou-et** [ru wɛ]  **jou-er** [ʒu we]

Exception    **ou** followed by **il** in the same syllable does not produce a glide but the vowel [u].  **mouille** [mu jə]

**oi**    produces [wa].
    **foi**     **roi**     **quoi**     **moi**     **soir**     **voir**

**oy**    followed by another vowel produces [waj].
    **voyage** [vwa ja ʒə]      **loyal**   [lwa jal]
    **voyez** [vwa je]         **moyen** [mwa jɛ̃]

    Occasionally in old spellings **oy** is final (*L'amour de moy*). In such cases it is pronounced simply [wa].

**oin**    produces [wɛ̃].
    **coin**    **soin**    **loin**    **foin**    **poindre**

*Glides*
[j]

[j] spelled

**i** followed by a vowel other than the neutral vowel produces either [j] or [ij] depending on the number of notes allotted to the sound group.

*one note:* **ciel** [sjɛl]   **bien** [bjɛ̃]   **fier** [fjɛr]
*one note:* **hier** [jɛr]   **précieux** [pre sjø]
*two notes:* **hi-er** [i jɛr]   **pré-ci-eux** [pre si jø]

**ï or y** also indicates the [j] glide.
**aïeux** [a jø]   **payer** [pɛ je]   **royal** [rwa jal]   **yeux** [jø]

**il** after a vowel, when the **il** is all within the same syllable, indicates [j].
**corail** [kɔ raj]   **soleil** [sɔ lɛj]

but **ai-le** [ɛ lə] (because the **i** and the **l** are in separate syllables).

**ill** after a vowel produces [j].
**aille** [a jə]   **abeille** [a bɛ jə]

after a consonant is pronounced [ij].
**fille** [fi jə]   **sillon** [si jõ]

Exceptions the common words **mille** [mi lə], **ville** [vi lə], **tranquille** [trɑ̃ ki lə] and their derivatives.
**million**   **millénaire**   **village**   **villanelle**
**villa**   **tranquillité**   **tranquilliser**

**ill** initial is pronounced [il].
**illusion** [i ly zjõ]   **illuminations** [i ly mi nɑ sjõ]

## Summary of glides

| [j] | [w] | [ɥ] |
|---|---|---|
| 1  **i** + vowel | 1  **ou** + vowel | 1  **u** + vowel |
| 2  **y** + vowel | 2  **oi** = [wa] | |
| 3  vowel + **il** = vowel + [j] | 3  **oin** = [wɛ̃] | |
| 4  vowel + **ill** = vowel + [j] | | |
| 5  cons. + **ill** = cons. + [ij] | | |
| except **mille ville** | | |
| **tranquille** | | |

## Combinations

interior **ai** = [ɛ]    **ay** = [ɛj]

        **oi** = [wa]    **oy** = [waj]

        **ui** = [ɥi]    **uy** = [ɥij]

## More words with the [j] glide

| | | | | | | | |
|---|---|---|---|---|---|---|---|
| **mieux** | [mjø] | **idiot** | [i djo] | **fiacre** | [fja krə] | **rien** | [rjɛ̃] |
| **sérieux** | [se rjø] or [se ri jø] | | | **mystérieuse** | [mi ste rjø zə] or [-ri jø zə] | | |
| **violon** | [vjɔ lõ] or [vi jɔ lõ] | | | **violet** | [vjɔ lɛ] or [vi jɔ lɛ] | | |
| **aïeul** | [a jœl] | **faïence** | [fa jɑ̃ sə] | **naïade** | [na ja də] | | |
| **crayon** | [krɛ jõ] | **loyer** | [lwa je] | **fuyons** | [fɥi jõ] | | |
| **émail** | [e maj] | **travail** | [tra vaj] | **sommeil** | [sɔ mɛj] | **vermeil** | [vɛr mɛj] |
| **oeil** | [œj] | **recueil** | [rə kœj] | **deuil** | [dœj] | **seuil** | [sœj] |
| **ailleurs** | [a jœr] | **bataille** | [ba tɑ jə] | **taille** | [tɑ jə] | | |
| **Mireille** | [mi rɛ jə] | **brouillard** | [bru jar] | **brouiller** | [bru je] | | |
| **mouiller** | [mu je] | **feuille** | [fœ jə] | **cueille** | [kœ jə] | **oeillet** | [œ jɛ] |
| **anguille** | [ɑ̃ gi jə] | **scintille** | [sɛ̃ ti jə] | **briller** | [bri je] | | |
| **habiller** | [a bi je] | **billet** | [bi jɛ] | **billard** | [bi jar] | | |
| **nasillard** | [na zi jar] | **carillon** | [ka ri jõ] | **papillon** | [pa pi jõ] | | |

CONSONANTS

1    Many final consonants are silent in French. Some are sounded.

2    All consonants within a word are sounded, except **h**, **m** before **n**, **m** and **n** when they indicate nasalization, and sometimes **p** before **t**.

3    French consonants should not be lingered over.

4    Double consonants (as in **année**, **occuper**, **appas**) should last no longer than single consonants. Unlike German and Italian they indicate no prolongation of sound.

5    Because of the non-phonetic nature of French spelling, consonants are grouped phonetically rather than in their alphabetical order. For a table of French sounds by their spelling see pages 167—169.

*Final consonants*
**b, c**

**b** is silent    when preceded by a nasal vowel.
**aplomb        plomb**

**b** is sounded    in all other cases.
**nabab        Mab        Jacob**

**c** is silent
    1    in
**estomac        tabac        croc        escroc**

    2    when preceded by a nasal vowel.
**banc        vainc        jonc**

Exceptions    **c** is sounded in some proper names.
**Poulenc** [pu lɛ̃k]        **Duparc**

**donc**    is usually pronounced [dɔ̃].
It is pronounced [dɔ̃k] in only three cases:

    1  Standing alone as an interjection.  **Donc!**

    2  At the beginning of a sentence or introducing a clause.
**Je pense, donc je suis.**
**Donc, pour me tenir compagnie...**(Carmen)
**Donc ce sera par un clair jour...**(Fauré)

    3  Before a word beginning with a vowel.
**Il était donc à Paris.**

**c** is sounded
    1    in
**arc        parc        turc**

    2    in all other words when preceded by vowel.
**lac        sec        estoc**

*Final consonants*
d, f, g, l, m, n, p, q


**d** is silent    **pied**    **nid**    **noeud**    **chaud**
              **coud**    **quand**    **vend**    **tard**
Exception    **sud** [syd]

**f** is sounded    **chef**  **bref**  **actif**  **boeuf**  **soif**
Exceptions    **clef** [kle]    **cerf** [sɛr]    **nerf** [nɛr]

**g** is silent    **sang**  **long**  **poing**  **bourg**  **faubourg**

**l** is usually silent    in words ending in **-il**.
              **fusil**  **gentil**  **sourcil**  **corail**
              **vermeil**  **seuil**  **orgueil**  **oeil**

**l** is sounded    in
              **avril**  **cil**  **exil**  **fil**  **il**  **myrtil**
              **subtil**  **péril**  **poil**  **vil**

              after all other vowels but **i**.
              **idéal**  **ciel**  **Israël**  **seul**
              **bol**  **nul**  **linceul**
Exception    **saoul** [su]

**m** is silent    **dam**  **faim**  **nom**  **parfum**
Exception    **album** [al bɔm]

**n** is silent    **ruban**  **mien**  **sein**  **fin**  **ton**  **brun**

**p** is silent    **champ**  **trop**  **coup**  **drap**  **galop**
Exceptions    **cap** [kap]  **cep** [sɛp]

**q** is sounded    as [k].    **coq** [kɔk]

*Final consonants*
**r**


r is usually sounded    **amer**     **enfer**     **hiver**     **mer**    **ver**     **venir**

                              **air**      **voir**     **fuir**      **pur**    **coeur**    **zéphyr**

**r** is silent    in the noun **baiser** [bɛ ze].

                in verbs in **-er**.
                **parler** [par le]     **aller** [a le]

                in words in **-ier**.
                **cahier**    [ka je]       **pommier** [pɔ mje]
                **premier** [prə mje]     **dernier**   [dɛr nje]
Exceptions    **fier**     **hier**

                words in **-yer**.
                **foyer** [fwa je]     **loyer** [lwa je]     **noyer** [nwa je]

                words in **-cher**.
                **archer** [ar ʃe]      **clocher** [klɔ ʃe]
                **rocher** [rɔ ʃe]      **cocher** [kɔ ʃe]
Exception    **cher** [ʃɛr]

                in words in **-ger**.
                **berger** [bɛr ʒe]     **léger**   [le ʒe]
                **danger** [dã ʒe]     **verger** [vɛr ʒe]

                in words in **-ailler, -eiller, -ouiller**.
                **poulailler** [pu lɑ je]     **oreiller** [ɔ rɛ je]     **houiller** [u je]

*Final consonants*
s

s is usually silent     suis     chantes     bas     livres     cyprès     cadis
                      confus     sous     encens     gens     alors     fais

s is sounded in     **fils** [fis] meaning *son* or *sons*.

                      **lys** and **fleur-de lys**, also spelled **lis**.

                      **jadis**     **hélas**     **iris**     **ours**

                      **os** (singular). (The plural **os** is [o].)

                      **sens** when it is a noun.
                      **Et nos sens extasiés** [e no sɑ̃ sɛk stɑ zje] (Verlaine)

                      **tous** when it is a pronoun.
                      **Moi seule, entre tous, je le brave** (Dalila)
                      [mwa sœl ɑ̃ trə tus ʒə lə bra və]

                      some personal and place names.
                      **Francis**     **St. Saëns**     **Damas**

                      many classical names.
                      **Atlas**     **Baucis**     **Damis**     **Tircis**
                      **Thaïs**     **Vénus**     **Mars**

**t** is usually silent   **chat**   **aspect** [a spɛ]   **finit**   **faut**   **doigt** [dwa]

Exceptions   **dot**   **est** (meaning **east**)
**Soit!** [swat] when it is used as an exclamation and means **So be it!**
(*Manon*, Acts I and II, *Carmen*, Act III)

**x** is usually silent   **faux**   **paix**   **choix**   **bijoux**

**z** is usually silent   **venez**  **chez**  **nez**   **assez**

Numbers   In the numbers **cinq**, **sept**, **huit**, **neuf** and **dix**, the final consonants
are pronounced when the words stand alone.
(When they are used as pronouns.)
**Il en avait cinq.** [i lɑ̃ na vɛ sɛ̃k]

These final consonants are silent when the numbers modify nouns.
**cinq livres** [sɛ̃ li vrə]

Loan-words   Many words which are non-French in origin (loan-words) do not
follow these rules. A few that might be encountered in a musical
setting have been noted in the preceding text.

Names   Many personal and place-names also do not follow these rules.
Some retain archaic pronunciations; others are foreign in origin.
For pronunciation of proper names, consult the Warnant dictionary.

To produce [b] and [p] clearly, the lips must be relaxed.

[b] is spelled
**b** and pronounced like English.

[p] is spelled
**b** when preceding an unvoiced consonant in the interior of a word.
**obtien** [ɔp tjɛ̃]    **absolu** [ap sɔ ly]    **subtil** [syp til]

**p** otherwise, and is pronounced like its Italian counterpart, i.e., dryly
and without a puff of air between it and a following vowel.

**p** is sounded at the beginning of a word, even if followed by another consonant.
**Psyché** [psi ʃe]

**p** is often silent when followed by **t** in the interior of a word.

| | | |
|---|---|---|
| **baptême** | **Baptiste** | |
| **sept** | **septième** | |
| **compter** | **comptable** | **compteur** |
| **dompter** | **domptage** | **dompteur** |
| **sculpture** | **sculpteur** | |

but sounded in

| | | | |
|---|---|---|---|
| **adopter** | **aptitude** | **conception** | **exapter** |
| **septembre** | **consomptif** | **consomption** | |
| **contemptable** | **présomptif** | **rédempteur** | **rédemption** |
| **somptueux** | | | |

**d** [d] **t** [t]  are dental as in Italian; that is, they are formed by placing the tip of the tongue against the back of the upper teeth. They are, however, not as dry as their Italian counterparts.

| dos | dé | dort | dans | don | des |
|-----|-----|------|------|-----|-----|
| tot | thé | tort | temps | ton | tes |

When [d] and [t] precede the sounds [i], [j], [y] and [ɥ], they are not dry at all; a small amount of air is allowed to pass between the tip of the tongue and the back of the teeth while the consonant is being articulated.

| dis | dieux | dure | réduire |
|-----|-------|------|---------|
| tire | tiens | tu | tuer |

Exception  **t** may sometimes sound like [s]. See page 207.

[f] spelled
**f** or **ph**  is effectively pronounced by placing the edge of the upper teeth behind the lower lip.

| faire | fond | face | fer | fanfare |
|-------|------|------|-----|---------|
| phare | phrase | prophète | pharmacie | Iphigénie |
| bref | chef | boeuf (but **boeufs** is [bø]) | | |
| | vif | oeuf (but **oeufs** is [ø]) | | |

Exceptions  **clef** [kle]  **nerf** [nɛr]

[v] spelled
**v** or **w**  is a voiced consonant and must have pitch. It is effectively produced by placing the upper teeth behind the lower lip.

| vive | vrai | avec | cave | vivace |
|------|------|------|------|--------|
| wagon | Watteau | Wallon | Wallonie | |

[g] is spelled

**g** when preceding **a**, **o**, **u** or a consonant.
**gai** **gout** **légume** **grand**

**gu** When **gu** is followed by another vowel, the **u** is silent:
**languir** [lɑ̃ gir] **guetter** [gɛ te]

Exception **aiguille** (needle) is [ɛ gɥi jə]

[ʒ] is spelled

**j** **je** **jaune**

**g** followed by **e**, **i** or **y**.
**gentil** **givre** **gymnase**

[ʒ] sounds like the **s** in **Persia**, **Asia**, but the sound is darker and richer.

[k] is spelled

**k** **kilomètre**

**qu** **quatre** **quel** (note that the **u** is silent)

**c** followed by **a**, **o**, **u** or a consonant.
**carte** **conte** **curé** **clos** **crus**

**ch** in words of Greek origin.
**archange** **Christ** **chrétien**
**choeur** **orchestre** **écho**

[ʃ] is spelled

**ch** It is the initial consonant sound in the English **shot**, but darker
and richer.
**chat** **charme** **chuchoter** **Psyché**

[r] The uvular **r**, although widely used in speech, should not be used in the singing of French (cabaret and music-hall singers excepted).

A double flip will usually suffice. Trilled **r** may be used for emphasis when it occurs in the first syllable of a word. **r** between vowels should not be trilled.

In order to sound, **r** must have a pitch; an **r** that is not clearly voiced (and therefore does not sound) may result in unexpected comedy (at best) or obscenity (at worst).

[l] is always forward and palatal.

[m] [n] **m** and **n** when sounded, are formed as in English. In singing it is important to remember that these consonants must receive a definite pitch in order to sound clearly. This pitch should be that of the vowel which follows.

**m, n** are silent when preceded by a vowel in the same syllable and serve only to indicate the nasality of the preceding vowel.
**maman** [ma mã]    **tombe** [tõ bə]

**m** is silent in the words **automne**, **damner**, **condamner**. The vowel preceding it is not nasalized.
[o tɔ nə]    [dɑ ne]    [kõ dɑ ne]

**mm, nn** are sounded as a single consonant with the vowel that follows. They usually cancel the nasal. Double consonants are not lengthened in French.
**comme** [kɔ mə]    **donner** [dɔ ne]

[ɲ] spelled **gn** is somewhat similar to the **ni** in English **onion**. For a more detailed description of this sound, see Page 77.
**agneau** [a ɲo]    **peigne** [pɛ ɲə]
**magnifique**    **magnétique**    **magnifier**    **oignon**
*206 French*

*Initial and interior consonants*
[s]

[s] is spelled

**s** beginning a word.
**sur** **soir**

within a word, except when it is between two vowels.
**ainsi** **esprit** **esclave** **aspect** [a spɛ]

at the end of a word in the rare cases when it is sounded. See page 201.

**ss** within a word.
**chasser** **classe**

**c** when it is followed by **e**, **i**, **y**.
**cette** **ciel** **cygne**

**ç** **garçon** **leçon**

**sc** when followed by **i** or **e**.
**scie** **science**

**ti** and is pronounced [sj] in many suffixes:

| | |
|---|---|
| **-tiable** | **insatiable**, **insatiablement** |
| **-tial(e)** | **initiale** (**-ment**) |
| **-tience** | **patience** [pa sjɑ̃ sə] |
| **-tient** | **patient** (but not **il tient**) |
| **-tieux** | **ambitieux** |
| **-tieuse** | **ambitieuse** |
| **-tion** | **nation**, **addition** |

Exception verbs ending in **-tions**.
**sortions** [sɔr tjõ]

*Initial and interior consonants*
[gz] [ks] [z]

[z] is spelled

**z**  **azure**

**s**  between two vowels (intervocalic).
**rose**  **briser**

**s** or **x**  when final in words where they are normally silent, take the sound [z] when they are elided to a following word beginning with a vowel.
**les amis** [lɛ za mi]  **deux amis** [dø za mi]

**x** is voiced [gz]  when between vowels or followed by **h**.
**exilé**  [ɛg zi le]  **existe**  [ɛg zi stə]
**exhale** [ɛg za lə]  **exhorter** [ɛg zɔr te]

Irregularities  **soixante** [swa sɑ̃ tə]  **deuxième** [dø zjɛ mə]
**sixième**  [si zjɛ mə]  **dixième**  [di zjɛ mə]

**x** is unvoiced [ks]  when followed by a consonant.
**extase** [ɛk stɑ zə]  **expédier** [ɛk spe dje]

in the following words and their derivatives:
**axis**  **complexion**  **complexité**  **élixir**  **fixer**
**luxe**  **relaxer**  **sexuel**  **taxi**  **vexer**

**cc**  before **e** or **i** is also pronounced [ks].
**accident** [ak si dɑ̃]  **accède** [ak sɛ də]

before other vowels it is simply [k].
**accabler** [a ka ble]  **accuser** [a ky ze]

*Orthographic* **h**

**h**   is always silent in French, whether initial (**homme**), or interior (**thé**, **exhaler**, **cahier**).

Often, final consonants may be elided to words beginning with **h**.
**les hommes** [lɛ zɔ mə]     **je suis heureuse** [ʒə sɥi zœ rø zə]

Other words beginning with **h** may **never** receive an elision. This **h** which acts as a barrier against elision, is known by the French as **h** *aspiré*, but it must be stressed that it is not sounded. Sounded initial **h** is considered a vulgarism.

**h** *aspiré*   Words beginning with **h** *aspiré* are marked in French dictionaries with an asterisk, an apostrophe or a little cross.
**haut** [*o]     or     ['o]     or     [⁺o]

The following are the most commonly encountered words beginning with **h** *aspiré*. Although one may never elide into these words (that is, sound a normally silent final consonant of a word preceding any of these words), it is not necessary to make a separation between the words by means of a glottal stop. The final vowel of the first word may still be linked to the first vowel of the second word.
**les/hautes** [lɛ o tə]

| | | | |
|---|---|---|---|
| ha! | halle | haricot | holà |
| hâbler | hallier | harnacher | homard |
| hache | halte | harpe | honte |
| hagard | hameau | hasard | hors |
| hai! | hampe | hâte | houle |
| haie | hanche | hausse | hucher |
| haillon | hanter | haut | huit |
| haine | happe | hautbois | hurler |
| haïr | harangue | hauteur | and derivatives, |
| halage | harasser | hennir | such as **honteux,** |
| haler | harceler | hérissé | **huitième, haïssable,** etc. |
| hâler | hardi | héros | |
| haleter | harangère | heurter | |

*209 French*

## Troublesome French words

Every language has a certain number of words in which, for one reason or another, the spelling does not seem to match the pronunciation. Fortunately French spelling, although complicated, is quite consistent, and the number of such words is relatively small, particularly in the poetic and dramatic vocabulary.

Here is a list of troublesome words frequently occurring in song and operatic texts.

| | | | |
|---|---|---|---|
| **aiguille** | [ɛ gɥi jə] | **mauvais** | [mɔ vɛ] |
| **boeuf, boeufs** | [bœf], [bø] | **monsieur** | [mə sjø] |
| **bonheur** | [bɔ nœr] | **messieurs** | [mɛ sjø] |
| **dessous, dessus** | [də su], [də sy] | **nerf** | [nɛr] |
| **donc** | [dõ] or [dõk] — see | **oeuf, oeufs** | [œf], [ø] |
| | page 198 | **oignon** | [ɔ ɲõ] |
| **est** (*east*) | [ɛst] | **os** (sing.) | [ɔs] |
| **eu, eût**, etc. | [y], [y], etc. | **ouest** | [wɛst] |
| **faisant**, etc. | [fə zã], etc. | **pays** | [pɛ ji] |
| **fils** (*son, sons*) | [fis] | **paysage** | [pɛ ji za ʒə] |
| **fils** (*threads*) | [fil] | **paysan** | [pɛ ji zã] |
| **femme** | [fa mə] | **prompt** | [prõ] |
| **fosse** | [fo sə] | **saoul, soûl** | [su] |
| **fossé** | [fo se] | **sens** (noun) | [sãs] |
| **grosse** | [gro sə] | **Soit!** (exclamation) | [swat] |
| **hélas** | [e lɑs] | **solennel** | [sɔ la nɛl] |
| **jadis** | [ʒa dis] | **sud** | [syd] |
| **Jésus Christ** | [ʒe zy kri] | **susure** | [sy sy rə] |
| **Le Christ** | [lə krist] | **tous** (pronoun) | [tus] |
| **lys, lis** | [lis] | **tous** (adjective) | [tu] |

ELISION

The subject of elision is a thorny one. Although there are certain cases where elision is required and other cases where one may never be made, there is a large gray area where elision is appropriate or not, depending on the circumstances. Long and intimate acquaintance with the French language is necessary before a reliable instinct is established.

Singers are referred to Pierre Bernac's excellent book **The Interpretation of French Song**. Besides several informative chapters about style, interpretation and diction, there are discussions of nearly two hundred French songs, with complete translations of the text, and indications where elision may or may not take place. A study of the examples will begin to give the singer a feeling for elision.

For operatic texts and for song texts not covered in Mr. Bernac's book, the following suggestions are offered as a guide.

*Pronunciation in elision*

The frequency of elision is far greater in singing than it is in normal conversational French.

[ə]  When a word ending in the neutral vowel [ə] is connected to a word beginning with a vowel, the [ə] is dropped completely.
**une âme** [y nɑ mə]    **la lune était** [la ly ne tɛ]

**s** and **x**  normally silent, take the sound [z] when they are sounded in elision.
**les amis** [lɛ za mi]    **deux amis** [dø za mi]

In the few cases where a final **s** is always sounded in a word, the **s** remains unvoiced when it is linked to the following word.
**Vénus et Mercure** [ve ny se mɛr ky rə]
**Et nos sens extasiés** [e no sɑ̃ sɛk sta zje] (*En sourdine*)

**d**  normally silent, takes the sound [t] in elision.
**Chacun de nous quand il buvait** [ʃa kœ̃ də nu kɑ̃ til by vɛ]
    (*Adieu, notre petite table*)
**À l'ombre d'un grand arbre** [a lõ brə dœ̃ grɑ̃ tar brə]
    (*Connais-tu le pays*)

**g**  normally silent, takes the sound [k] in elision.
**sang impur** [sɑ̃ kɛ̃ pyr] (*Marseillaise*)
**long hiver** [lõ ki vɛr]
**d'un long exil** [dœ̃ lõ kɛg zil] (*Voici que le printemps*)

**léger, premier**  normally pronounced with closed [e] in the second syllable [le ʒe, prə mje], change to [ɛ] in elision.
**un léger ennui** [œ̃ le ʒɛ rɑ̃ nɥi]
**le premier homme** [lə prə mjɛ rɔ mə]

Nasality  Some nasal vowels keep and some lose their nasality in elision.

[ɑ̃]  always remains nasal.
**en avant** [ɑ̃ na vɑ̃]

*212 French*

[ɛ̃]

1 loses nasality in the endings **-ain** and **-ein**.
    **certain auteur** [sɛr tɛ no tœr]    **un vain espoir** [œ̃ vɛ nɛ spwar]
    **en plein air** [ã plɛ nɛr]

2 loses nasality in the words **ancien, moyen, divin**.
    **un ancien ami** [œ̃ nã sjɛ na mi]    **moyen Âge** [mwa jɛ nɑ ʒə]
    **le divin Enfant** [lə di vi nã fã]

3 remains nasal in all other cases. **bien-aimé** [bjɛ̃ nɛ me]

[õ] loses nasality only in the word **bon**.
    **bon élève** [bɔ ne lɛ və]    **bonheur** [bɔ nœr]    **bonhomme** [bɔ nɔ mə]

[œ̃] always remains nasal. **un ami** [œ̃ na mi]

**rd, rs, rt** When a word ends in **rd, rs** or **rt** the **r** is elided to the following word, omitting **d, s** or **t**.
    **D'abord indécise et timide** [da bɔ rɛ̃ de si ze ti mi də]
        (**Carmen** *Chanson de Bohême*)
    **Me penchant vers elle** [mə pã ʃã vɛ rɛ lə] (*Poème de l'amour*)
    **Cela ne sert à rien** [sə la nə sɛ ra rjɛ̃] (**Carmen** *Card aria*)
    **O sort amer** [o sɔ ra mɛr] (*Absence*)
    **De chaque branche part une voix** [də ʃa kə brã ʃə pa ry nə vwa]
        (*La lune blanche*)

Exceptions But when a pronoun follows a verb ending in **rd** or **rt** the final consonant is elided.
    **Que perd-on?** [kə pɛr tõ]    **Quand part-on?** [kɑ par tõ]

In words ending in **rs**, when the **s** indicates a plural, it is elided.
    **Aux cœurs amoureux** [o kœr za mu rø] (*Printemps qui commence*)
    **Laisse ces desirs éphémères** [lɛ sə sɛ de zir ze fe mɛ rə]
        (*Voyons, Manon*)
    **Si mes vers avaient des ailes** [si me vɛr za ve dɛ zɛ lə]

*When to elide*

Words which relate to each other in meaning or which modify each other are generally linked together.

Elide between

1   an article and the following word.
    **un ami** [œ̃ na mi]     **aux amis** [o za mi]
    **les amis** [lɛ za mi]
    **un assez grand nombre** [œ̃ na se grɑ̃ nõ brə]

2   an adjective and its noun.
    **mon ami** [mõ na mi]     **cet homme** [sɛ tɔ mə]
    **deux amis** [dø za mi]     **un doux accord** [œ̃ du za kɔr]
    **Sous ces tranquilles ombrages** [su se trɑ̃ ki lə zõ bra ʒə]
        (*Le rêve*)

When the noun precedes the adjective, an elision is made in the plural.
    **Grinçaient sous les mains obstinées** [grɛ̃ sɛ su lɛ mɛ̃ zɔp sti ne ə]
        (Carmen *Chanson de Bohême*)

Exception   *not* in the singular.
    **Enfant / abandonnée** [ɑ̃ fɑ̃ a bɑ̃ dɔ ne ə] (*Il est doux, il est bon*)
    **Loin du pays / aimé** [lwɛ̃ dy pɛ ji ɛ me] (*Au cimitière*)

3   a verb and its adverb or adverbial phrase.
    **Brillent au firmament** [bri jə to fir ma mɑ̃] (*Lève-toi soleil*)
    **Nous n'avons encor que vingt ans** [nu na võ zɑ̃ kɔr kə vɛ̃ tɑ̃]
        (Manon *Gavotte*)
    **Les étoffes flottaient au vent** [lɛ ze tɔ fə flɔ tɛ to vɑ̃]
        (Carmen *Chanson de Bohême*)
    **Cent hommes marchent à sa suite** [sɑ̃ tɔ mə mar ʃə ta sa sɥi tə]
        (Carmen *Card trio*)

4   an adverb and a following adjective.
    **je suis heureuse, trop heureuse** [ʒə sɥi zœ rø zə tro pœ rø zə]
        (*Depuis le jour*)
    **Tout emplie de mystère** [tu tɑ̃ pli də mi stɛ rə] (*Shéhérazade*)
    **Si doucement enclos** [si du sə mɑ̃ tɑ̃ klo] (*De fleurs*)
*214 French*

5     a preposition and a following word; a negative and a following word.
       **Dans une coupe amère** [dɑ̃ zy nə ku pa mɛ rə]     (Werther)
       **Sous un ciel toujours bleu** [su zœ̃ sjɛl tu ʒur blø] (Mignon)
       **Pas un seul témoignage** [pɑ zœ̃ sœl te mwa ɲa ʒə]     (Werther)

6     a subject with its verb.
       **Vous avez** [vu za ve]
       **En elles, tout est séduisant** [ɑ̃ nɛ lə tu tɛ se dɥi zɑ̃] (*Voyons, Manon*)
       **Où les silences ont les voix** [u lɛ si lɑ̃ sə zɔ̃ lɛ vwa] (*Notre amour*)

7     compound subjects, objects, verbs.
       **Les cartes et les dés nous attendent** [lɛ kar tə ze lɛ de nu za tɑ̃ də]
          (Manon Act I)
       **Amour, viens aider ma faiblesse** [a mur vjɛ̃ ze de ma fɛ blɛ sə]
       **Que de villes et de hameaux** [kə də vi lə ze də a mo] (*Absence*)

8     two adjectives modifying the same noun.
       **Les clairs et joyeux ruisseaux** [lɛ klɛr ze ʒwa jø rɥi so] (*Le rêve*)

9     a verb and its object.
       **Portait un collier de grains d'or** [pɔr tɛ tœ̃ kɔ lje də grɛ̃ dɔr]
          (*Voyons, Manon*)
       **L'amour est enfant de Bohême** [la mu rɛ tɑ̃ fɑ̃ də bɔ ɛ mə]
          (Carmen *Habanera*)
       **Dansent une ronde folle** [dɑ̃ sə ty nə rɔ̃ də fɔ lə] (*Le veau d'or*)

10     the infinitive ending **-er** is elided in singing although it is not elided
      in speech.
       **...me donner un tel rêve** [mə dɔ ne rœ̃ tɛl rɛ və] (*Vision fugitive*)
       **Qu'à jeter un regard sur moi** [ka ʒə te rœ̃ rə gar syr mwa]
          (Carmen *Flower Song*)
       **Aimer, aimer et mourir** [ɛ me ɛ me re mu rir] (*Connais-tu le pays*)
       **Et troubler à jamais** [e tru ble ra ʒa mɛ] (*Elle ne croyait pas*)

*When not to elide*

Do not elide

1 when a word is followed by a mark of punctuation.
  **Mais, / ô mon bien-aimé** [mɛ o mõ bjɛ̃ nɛ me]
   (*Mon coeur s'ouvre à ta voix*)
  **Eut, / en souvenir de sa belle** [y ɑ̃ su və nir də sa bɛ lə]
   (*Le roi de Thulé*)
  **Seules, / en plein soleil** [sœ lə ɑ̃ plɛ̃ sɔ lɛj] (*Phidylé*)

2 when for clarity of meaning or interpretation, a pause is desirable
 after a word. In other words, if a comma can be inserted, do not elide.
  **Dans les grands jours / il s'en servait** [dɑ̃ lɛ grɑ̃ ʒur il sɑ̃ sɛr vɛ]
   (*Le roi de Thulé*)
  **Et doucement / il rendit l'âme** [e du sə mɑ̃ il rɑ̃ di lɑ mə]
   (*Le roi de Thulé*)
  **Elle / à la mer, nous / au tombeau** [ɛl a la mɛr nu o tõ bo]
   (*Beau soir*)

3 in general when words do not modify each other or have no
 grammatical connection.
  **Les nuages effarouchés / ont disparu** [lɛ nɥaʒ ze fa ru ʃe õ di spa ry]
   (*Le cygne*)
  In this example the adjective **effarouchés** modifies the noun **nuages**,
  not the verb **ont disparu.**

  **Joignez-vous / aux zéphirs** [ʒwa ɲe vu o ze fir] (*Diane et Actéon*)
   The adverbial phrase **aux zéphirs** modifies the verb **joignez,**
   not the pronoun **vous.**

4    from a noun or pronoun into a preposition.

**Il faisait les doux yeux / à Manon** [il fə zɛ lɛ du zjø a ma nõ]

**Qui me rafraîchissaient le front avec des palmes** [ki mə ra frɛ ʃi
se lə frõ a vɛk dɛ pal mə] (*La vie antérieure*)

This rule would also apply to the last examples of 2 and 3 above.

Exception    But it is possible to make this elision in cases where the prepositional
phrase is descriptive of the noun.

**Des habits à longues franges** [dɛ za bi za lõ gə frã ʒə] (*Shéhérazade*)

**J'ai des galants à la douzaine** [ʒe dɛ ga lã za la du zɛ nə]
(Carmen *Séguedille*)

**Beaux yeux à flammes douces** [bo zjø za flɑ mə du sə]
(*Puisque l'aube grandit*)

5    when the second word begins with **h** *aspiré*. See page 209.

**...opinion trop / haute** [ɔ pi ɲõ tro o tə] (Manon Act I)

**Sans amour et sans / haine** [sã za mu re sã ɛ nə]
(*Il pleure dans mon coeur*)

**Que les branches / hautes font** [kə lɛ brã ʃə o tə fõ] (*En sourdine*)

6    when the second word is **oui**, or the first word is **et**.

**mais / oui**       **parents‿et / amis** [pa rã ze a mi]

7    when the second word is a number.

**ses / onze enfants**    **deux cent / un**    **les numéros / un**

Exception    But **les‿uns** is possible where **uns** is a pronoun, not a number.

**Il est‿onze heures** is also possible.

8    when a noun ends in a nasal vowel.

**Car une belle enfant / était sur le rivage** (*Poeme de l'amour*)

**Le vent / a changé** (*Le temps des lilas*)

**Le dernier rayon / agonise** (*Soir*)

**Reste un moment / ici**

*217 French*

Here is a check list of errors commonly made in French by American singers. If you are told that "your French does not sound very French", consider each of these points. Your error may lie in one or more of these areas.

1   *Are you singing a true legato?*  A perfect legato may be the most difficult thing for Americans to achieve in French. In English we are accustomed to a stop-and-go articulation which does not exist in French. This articulation of ours is sometimes so subtle, and we are so accustomed to it, that we do not realize how non-legato it is. For example, in listening to someone speak, we would have no difficulty in differentiating between **mend raw** and **men draw**; there is a subtle halt in the flow between the words. In French this halt does not take place.

This linking together of words is but one aspect of the French legato. The basis of it lies, of course, in the length of the vowels. Consonants must be delayed in their articulation as long as possible. Keep the vowel sound alive and pure. The listener should never be aware of an oncoming consonant. Articulation of consonants must be brief, neat and clear. French, like Italian, goes from vowel to vowel. But French is even smoother, for it does not have the prolonged double consonant sounds of Italian.

No matter how accurate your pronunciation may be, it will not "sound French" if it is not super-smooth.

2   *Do your vowels keep the same quality from beginning to end?*  In English we slide in and out of vowels, and each time we open our mouths to speak, we are practicing this bad habit. Form the vowels simultaneously with the consonants preceding them. That will eliminate a glide-in. Do not move lips, tongue or jaw while sustaining a vowel. That will eliminate a glide-off.

3 *Are your high vowels high enough and your round vowels round enough?* Special attention should be given to [e], [o], [y], [ø] and [œ].

4 *Do you sound an* **m** *or* **n** *in nasal vowels?* This is a particularly bad habit of American singers. It is most apt to occur in words like **sombre** or **onde** where a **b** or **d** follows the nasal. Often singers who are sounding the **m** or **n** do not realize that they are doing so.

5 *Are the nasal vowels too nasal?* Nasality should not be forced. Do not "sing in the nose". Remember that a nasal vowel is a normal oral vowel which has had some nasal resonance added to it. Do you have enough nasality in the nasal vowels? Don't be afraid of the nasal resonance. With a little practice good nasal vowels can be achieved without pinching the tone as long as their basis is a good [ɑ], [ɛ], [o] or [œ].

6 *Are you using the bright French* [a]*?* The tendency for young singers is to sing **ah** too darkly in all languages. Remember that in French, most **ah**'s are even brighter than they would be in English, Italian or German. The bright sound of [a] is highly characteristic of French.

7 *Are you accurate in the French neutral vowel* [ə]*?* Many Americans substitute the vowel [ʌ] (as in the English **up**). This vowel does not exist in French.

8 *Do you produce the consonant sounds* [ʃ] *and* [ʒ] *with a rich quality,* or do they sound shallow?

9 *Is it clear?* If French is not clear it will not "sound French" no matter how accurately you may think you are pronouncing. Clarity is not to be achieved by spitting out words, but by an untroubled legato line created by smoothly flowing clear vowels and gracefully articulated consonants.

# German

This section is intended as a guide to the singing pronunciation of German. The rules quoted here follow common stage practice in Germany and Austria and reflect the usage of the outstanding German singers of our time. They do not necessarily apply to idiomatic conversational German. Fortunately there are many recordings available of singers whose diction is outstandingly clear and refined—Dietrich Fischer-Dieskau, Hermann Prey, Erna Berger and Christa Ludwig, to mention a few. These singers should be studied as models of clarity, style and projection.

*Dictionaries*

1961     Langenscheidt's Pocket German Dictionary. New York: Barnes & Noble (English-German, German-English) The pocket edition, retailing for under $5.00, uses the IPA alphabet. Some more expensive editions of Langenscheidt do not.

The paper-back edition of Langenscheidt published in 1972 by Pocket Books uses IPA. Earlier editions of the paper-back do not.

1973     Cassell's Compact German-English Dictionary. New York: Dell Books. The paper-back edition uses IPA.

**Siebs, Theodor**    1961     Deutsche Hochsprache, Bühnenaussprache. Berlin: Walter de Gruyter & Co. (German only) The word-list section has many proper names and other words of non-German origin.

*Dictionary transcriptions*

Note: The Langenscheidt dictionary notates differences between open and closed vowels in all cases except those involving spelled **i**, **u** and **ü**. With these three vowels it notates only difference in length and does not utilize the symbols [I], [U] and [Y]. With these three letters a colon after the phonetic symbol indicates a long vowel (closed); absence of the colon indicates a short vowel (open).

| | *Langenscheidt* | *IPA* |
|---|---|---|
| i | [i:] (long) | [i] (closed) |
| i | [i] (short) | [I] (open) |
| u | [u:] (long) | [u] (closed) |
| u | [u] (short) | [U] (open) |
| ü (or **y**) | [y:] (long) | [y] (closed) |
| ü (or **y**) | [y] (short) | [Y] (open) |

**Cassell's New Compact Dictionary** indicates the difference between [i] and [I]. But it follows the Langenscheidt system in regard to [u], [U], [y] and [Y].

Umlaut  Any umlauted vowel may also be spelled without the umlaut by adding an **e** after the vowel.
**Jaeger = Jäger      schoen = schön      ueber = über**

The pronounciation is the same in both spellings.

ß  is a ligature equivalent to **ss**.

th  which exists only in old spelling, should be counted as one consonant.
**roth = rot** [rot]      **Blüthen = Blüten** [bly tən]      **Goethe** [gø tɛ]

VOWELS

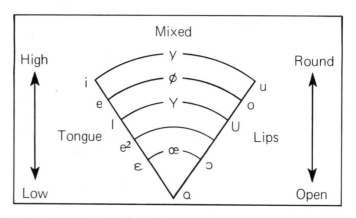

Nearly every German vowel in the sung language has two sounds:

|  | closed | open |  | closed | open |
|---|---|---|---|---|---|
| **a** | [ɑ] | [ɑ] | **o** | [o] | [ɔ] |
| **ä** or **ae** | [e²] | [ɛ] | **ö** or **oe** | [ø] | [œ] |
| **e** | [e] | [ɛ] | **u** | [u] | [U] |
| **i** | [i] | [I] | **ü** or **ue** | [y] | [Y] |
| **ie** | [i] | — | **y** | [y] | [Y] |

In spoken German vowels are considered according to quantity (long and short) as well as quality (open and closed). In singing consideration is given mainly to quality because duration is, in the main, determined by the composer. Although differentiation, therefore, is made in speaking between long [ɑ] and short [ɑ], none can be made in singing. Only the [ɑ] in English **father** or Italian **alma** is used. Similarly, a word like **Welt**, spoken with a short, open vowel may occur in a musical setting on a long, sustained note. Although the vowel in such a case must be long, it still must be open.

*Closed vowels*

[e] spelled is equivalent to French closed **e** as in **parler**. It is closely related in sound and in position to [i].

    e   **leben**

   ee   **Meer**

   eh   **mehr**

$[e^2]$ spelled is equivalent to closed Italian **e** (relaxed closed **e**) as in **vero**.

   ä   **Tränen**

[i] spelled is equivalent to the vowel in English **seen**.

   i   **wir**

   ie   **Liebe**

   ih   **ihn**

[o] spelled is equivalent to French closed **o** as in **beau**. It is closely related in sound and position to [u].

   o   **tot**

   oo   **Boot**

   oh   **Sohn**

[ø] spelled is a composite of [o] and [e]. It is formed by shaping the lips for [o] and pronouncing [e]. It is equivalent to the vowel in French **feu**.

   ö   **schön**

   öh   **Söhne**

[u] spelled is equivalent to the vowel in English **moon**.

   u   **Buch**

   uh   **Uhr**

[y] spelled is a composite of [u] and [i].
It is formed by shaping the lips for [u] and pronouncing [i].
It is equivalent to the vowel in French **tu**.

   ü   **Tür**

   üh   **führen**

   y   **Zypresse**

*Open vowels*

[ɛ] spelled    is equivalent to the vowel in English **red**.
     e    **Bett**
     ä    **hätte**

[I] spelled    is equivalent to the vowel in English **sin**.
     i    **bin**

[ɔ] spelled    is equivalent to the vowel in the English **cough**.
     o    **Sonne**

[œ] spelled    is equivalent to the vowel in the French **coeur**. It is a composite
of [ɔ] and [ɛ] and is formed by shaping the lips for
[ɔ] and pronouncing [ɛ].
     ö    **Hölle**

[U] spelled    is equivalent to the vowel in English **foot**.
     u    **Mutter**

[Y] spelled    is a composite of two vowels. It is formed by shaping the lips for
[U] and pronouncing [I]. It has no equivalent in English or French.
     ü    **füllen**
     y    **Myrten**

*Neutral vowels*

German employs a neutral, or obscure, vowel [ə] for certain cases where **e** occurs in an unstressed position. In the spoken language most unstressed **e**'s may be pronounced [ə]. In sung German, however, this is not the case. Although there seem to be three or four differing systems of rules governing the pronunciation of unstressed **e**, the following system seems to be the one in the widest use.

1   For prefixes, use open **e** [ɛ].
**vergeht** [fɛr get]

2   If **e** is the final letter in the word, a bright neutral vowel should be used. This is "open **e**", but not stressed [ɛ].
**Liebe** [li bɛ]      **leise** [lɑ:Izɛ]

3   The dark neutral vowel [ə] should be used for any unstressed **e** occurring after the stressed vowel when that **e** is followed by a consonant. (**e** post-stress, followed by a consonant)
**Leben** [le bən]

For a discussion of the sound of [ə], see page 21.

1 For our purposes a root-stem may be defined as that part of a word which gives it its basic meaning, its identity. In the word series **love**, **lov**ing, **lov**er, **lov**ed, **lov**ely, for instance, the smallest common denominator is **lov-**. This is a root-stem which we use as a label for a specific concept. Letters occuring after this root-stem modify the basic meaning in one way or another.

2 In German, **lieb-** is a root-stem and may be found in the words **Lieb**e, **lieb**end, **Lieb**chen, **lieb**te, **lieb**lich. These words all refer to the same basic concept but have varying shades of meaning.

3 For contraction in root-stems, see page 241.

4 Stress in German

*In native words* the principal stress nearly always falls on the first syllable of the root-stem.

**Lieb**e  **Lieb**chen  ver**lieb**e  **Kön**ig  **Kön**igin  **kön**iglich

*In loan words* (words of non-German origin) the stress is unpredictable.

**Melodie**  **Musik**  **Zypresse**  **Akkord**

*In compound words* when two or more roots are combined, the primary stress falls on the first syllable of the first root. Weak secondary stresses occur on the first syllable of the other roots.

**Mondeslicht**  **liebestrunkene**  **wegzufliehn**

In compound adverbs the stress falls on the second root.

**zurück**  **hinweg**  **heraus**  **hinauf**  **vorüber**

In **allein** and **warum** the stress falls on the second root.

The adjective **lebendig** is irregular, the stress falling after the root-stem.

The negative prefix **un-** usually receives the stress.

**unschuldig**  **unvertraut**  **unglücklich**

*Vowel quality
in root stems*

In order to identify the quality of a vowel (open or closed) in verbs, nouns and adjectives, it is necessary to identify root-stems. The quality of the stressed vowel is determined by the number of consonants following it in the root-stem.

Verbs    Trace the verb back to its infinitive (**lebte** = **leben**). When the **-en** infinitive ending is dropped, what remains is the root-stem (**leb-**).

1    When a vowel is closed in the infinitive root-stem, it is often closed throughout all forms.

**reg**en [e]    **reg**t [e]    **geb**en [e]    **gib**t [i]
**wander**n    **wandel**n    **forder**n    **sammel**n

2    Unstressed prefixes are not considered part of the root-stem. That they are unstressed may be determined by reciting the musical setting aloud in rhythm.

ge**geb**en    ver**lieb**te    ent**floss**en

3    Remember that verbs with separable prefixes are made up of two roots. The primary stress will fall on the first of the two.

auf**nehm**en    ausge**flog**ener    fort**geh**en

Nouns and adjectives    The root-stem is the shortest common denominator of the dictionary form, minus any final vowel.

**Welt**    **Lieb**e    **König**in    **rund**    **fremd**

With the exception of a few monosyllabic words (**Au**, **See**, **lau**, **so**, **zu**, etc.) German roots end in consonants.

Other parts of speech    It is not necessary to trace root-stems. Prepositions, pronouns, articles, adverbs, etc. are considered in toto.

Closed vowels (with the exception of unstressed final **o**) occur only in stressed syllables. In other words, in root-stems, or in the first syllable of multi-syllable roots. In words of foreign derivation, closed vowels may occur in unstressed syllables.

**Zypresse** [tsy prɛs:sɛ]     **Melodie** [me lo di]

Vowels are closed

1   when final in a monosyllabic word.
**wo** [o]     **je** [e]     **zu** [u]     **so** [o]     **du** [u]

2   when final and stressed.
**Ade** [e]     **Juche** [e]

3   when doubled.
**Meer** [e]     **See** [e]     **Seele** [e]     **Beet** [e]     **Boot** [o]     **Moos** [o]

4   when followed by **h**.
**spähn** [e²]     **mehr** [e]     **ihr** [i]     **Sohn** [o]
**Höhle** [ø]     **früh** [y]     **ruhen** [u]

5   when followed by only one consonant in the root-stem.

| Rät | wer | wir | rot | schön | Hut | für |
|---|---|---|---|---|---|---|
| trägst | schwebt | gibt | gelobt | schönste | mutlos | Blümlein |
| täglich | regt | gibst | geholt | hörte | tust | lügst |

6   in the nouns **Mond, Obst, Trost, Wüste** and the adjectives **gross** and **hoch** and their derivatives **Tröster, grösseste, höchst, Höchster**, etc.

**Hochzeit**   The noun **Hochzeit** (wedding) is pronounced with open **o**. [ɔ]

**e** is closed      [e] in:
**Erde   erst   Erz   Herd   Pferd   Schwert   stets   wert   werden**

**o** is closed      when unstressed and final.
**also** [o]     **jetzo** [o]     **Tamino** [o]     **Papageno** [o]     **Echo** [o]

**sein**      is highly irregular in pronunciation:
**bin** [bIn]     **bist** [bIst]     **ist**    [Ist]     **sind**     [zInt
**seid** [za:It]     **wäre** [ve²rɛ]     **wärest** [ve²rɛst]     **gewesen** [gɛ ve zən]

**werden**      The stressed vowel is closed in the present tense (**werde, wirst, werd,** etc.) but open in other tenses (**wurde, geworden,** etc.).

**Weg**      uses closed **e** when it is a noun (*road*), but open **e** when it is an adverb (*away*).

Stressed **u, ü + ch**      is usually closed.
**Buch** [u]     **Tuch** [u]     **Fluch** [u]     **kuchen** [u]
**Bücher** [y]     **Tücher** [y]     **Flüche** [y]

but occasionally open.
**Bucht** [U]     **Luchs** [U]     **Wuchs** [U]

A way to remember this rule is:
     After **u** or **ü**, **ch** counts as one consonant.

Vowels are open

1   when stressed and followed by two or more consonants in the root-stem.

| | | | | |
|---|---|---|---|---|
| <u>Wellen</u> [ɛ] | <u>recht</u> [ɛ] | <u>will</u> [I] | <u>Bilder</u> [I] | <u>Händen</u> [ɛ] |
| <u>doch</u> [ɔ] | <u>Volk</u> [ɔ] | <u>Kunde</u> [U] | <u>höllisch</u> [œ] | ge<u>füllt</u> [Y] |
| <u>immer</u> [I] | <u>ich</u> [I] | <u>Myrten</u> [Y] | <u>fort</u> [ɔ] | <u>rund</u> [U] |

2   in the following prepositions and monosyllables:

| | |
|---|---|
| **bin** | **ob** |
| **bis** | **um, darum, warum** |
| **es** | **un-** (negative prefix) |
| **des** | **von, vom** |
| **hin** | **wes** |
| **in, im** | **zum** |
| **mit** | |

Note that **vor** [for] is not in this list and is regular.

3   in the unstressed prefixes **be-, emp-, ent-, er-, ge-, ver-, zer-**.

**behalten**    **empfangen**      **entgegen**     **erhalten**
**gegangen**    **verschwiegen**   **zerrissen**

Exception    Siebs advocates use of the neutral vowel [ə] for the prefixes **ge-** and **be-**, [ɛ] for the remaining. There seems to be a wide variation among German singers in the pronunciation of the prefixes. Some singers pronounce them all with [ɛ], others use [ɛ] and [ə], some even use [ə] exclusively. For consistency, and for better projection and clarity, [ɛ] is advised for all prefixes in sung German.

4   **o** and **u** followed by **ss** (**ß**).

Although the presence of two consonants after a vowel usually indicates that the vowel is to be pronounced open (as in **doppel**, **Himmel**, **Mutter**, etc.), there are many words in which **o**, **ö**, **u**, **ü** should be pronounced closed when followed by double **s**.

| *closed* | | *open* | |
|---|---|---|---|
| | **Schoß** (lap) | | **Schoß** (sprout) |
| | **Schloße** (hailstone) | | **Schloß** (castle) |
| | **süss** | | **Kuss, küssen** |
| | **bloss** | | **muss, müssen** |
| | **goss** | | **Schluss** |
| | **gross, grösste** | | **Fluss, Flüssen** |
| | **Gruss, grüssen** | | |
| | **Fuss** | | |

Since **o**, **ö**, **u**, **ü** followed by **ss** are unpredictable, consult the dictionary in each case.

## DIPHTHONGS AND GLIDES

German has three diphthongs with five spellings.

**ai, ei** [ɑːI]   **Hain, Pein**       Similar to English **mine**.

**au** [ɑːU]   **Baum**          Similar to English **cow**.

**eu, äu** [ɔːy]   **treu, träumen**   Similar to English **boy**.

As in English and Italian, care must be taken to prolong the first vowel of the diphthong; the second vowel is merely a glide-off.

**j** [j]   is the only glide in German. It is equivalent to French [j] as in **Dieu** [djø]. It is very forward and palatial and has more buzz than its English counterpart as found in **yes**.

The glide [j] must have a pitch or it will sound like [ç] (as in the German **ich**).

| | | | | | |
|---|---|---|---|---|---|
| **ja** | [jɑ] | **Jahr** | [jɑr] | **jeder** | [je dər] |
| **Jüngling** | [jYŋ lIŋ] | **Jagd** | [jɑkt] | **jung** | [jUŋ] |
| **Jäger** | [je² gər] | **jauchzen** | [jɑːUx tsən] | | |

**ie**   in unstressed syllables of some loan-words will produce [jɛ].
   **Lilie** [li ljɛ]     **Familie** [fɑ mi ljɛ]

*An exercise in double consonants*

| | | | | | |
|---|---|---|---|---|---|
| **Locken** | [lɔk:kən] | **wecken** | [vɛk:kən] | **schmecken** | [ʃmɛk:kən] |
| **Waffen** | [vɑf:fən] | **alle** | [ɑl:lɛ] | **fallen** | [fɑl:lən] |
| **Himmel** | [hIm:məl] | **immer** | [Im:mər] | **nimmer** | [nIm:mər] |
| **Schlummer** | [ʃlUm:mər] | **Lippen** | [lIp:pən] | **doppel** | [dɔp:pəl] |
| **girren** | [gIr:rən] | **knurren** | [knUr:rən] | **besser** | [bɛs:sər] |
| **küssen** | [kYs:sən] | **wissen** | [vIs:sən] | **Messer** | [mɛs:sər] |
| **retten** | [rɛt:tən] | **Schatten** | [ʃɑt:tən] | **Ketten** | [kɛt:tən] |

CONSONANTS

Consonant sounds in German are incisive and intense. Voiced consonants must be clearly pitched.

In sung German all written consonants must be pronounced. This rule has only one exception—**h** in certain positions. (See page 246) **r**, which is sometimes dropped in spoken German, must always be sounded in the sung language.

Although some German grammarians do not recognize the existence of lengthened double consonant sounds (in the same enthusiastic way that the Italians do), others insist that double consonants must be lengthened in sound to give the effect of shortened vowels preceding them. This is especially important in the sustained diction of singing and will often prevent a confusion between two similar words of disparate meaning.

| | |
|---|---|
| **ihre** | **irre** |
| **her** | **Herr** |
| **Schal** | **Schall** |
| **hehren** | **Herren** |
| **fühlen** | **füllen** |
| **bieten** | **bitten** |
| **Höhle** | **Hölle** |

Excellent examples of lengthened double consonants will be found in the many recordings by Dietrich Fischer-Dieskau.

*Final consonants*
**b, d, g, s**

b, **d**, **g** and **s** are unvoiced when they occur in certain positions.

**b** is pronounced [p]
**d** is pronounced [t]
**g** is pronounced [k]
**s** is pronounced [s]

1  at the ends of words, either in single words or in compounds.

| | | | | | | |
|---|---|---|---|---|---|---|
| **Laub** [lɑːUp] | **mild** [mIlt] | **Tag** [tɑk] | **Gans** [gɑns] |
| **ob** [ɔp] | **Land** [lɑnt] | **Weg** [vek] | **uns** [uns] |
| **Liebkosen** [lip koː zən] | | **Landschaft** [lɑnt ʃaft] | |
| **Wegweiser** [vekvɑːIzər] | | **Halsband** [hɑlsbɑnt] | |

2  in a final consonant cluster.

| | | |
|---|---|---|
| **geliebt** [gɛlipt] | **bleibt** [blɑːIpt] | **bebst** [bepst] |
| **Magd** [mɑkt] | **regt** [rekt] | **bewegt** [bɛvekt] |
| **Jagd** [jɑkt] | **Dunst** [dUnst] | **hörst** [hørst] |

3  at the end of a root-stem when followed by another consonant.

| | |
|---|---|
| **glaublich** [glɑːUplIç] | **lieblich** [liplIç] |
| **Rädlein** [re²tlɑːIn] | **Mädchen** [me²tçən] |
| **endlich** [ɛntlIç] | **sagbar** [zɑkbɑr] |
| **Täubchen** [tɔːypçən] | **sagt** [zɑkt] |
| **Bildnis** [bIltnIs] | **Feigling** [fɑːIklіŋ] |

*Contractions*

**d** in contraction

1    In some two-syllable roots, a contraction may take place:
**wandle** from **wandeln**; **andre** from **ander**, etc.

In these examples the **d** is not at the end of the root-stem, so it should not be unvoiced. A similar case would arise with **wandre** (from **wandern**).   [vɑndrɛ] not [vɑntrɛ]

2    It is also possible for a contraction to take place in the suffixes. For example, **goldenen** may be contracted to **goldnen**. The **d** in **goldnen** should not be unvoiced, even though the vowel originally following it has been omitted. A similar contraction may take place when nouns are made into verbs, e.g., the verb **segnen** from **Segen**.

**goldnen** [gɔldnən] not [gɔltnən]
**holdner** [hɔldnər]       **Röslein** [røzlɑːɪn]
**segnen**  [zegnən]       **regnen**  [regnən]

Remember that **dn** is not a consonant succession that usually occurs in single German words. The same is true of **gn**.

**ch** is hard [x] after **a**, **o**, **u** and **au**.

**Nacht** [nɑxt]     **Bach** [bɑx]     **Fluch** [flux]     **suchen** [zu xən]
**pochen** [pɔ xən]     **doch** [dɔx]     **auch** [ɑ:Ux]     **Rauch** [rɑ:Ux]

The sound [x] must never be confused with the sound [k].

| [x] | [k] | [x] | [k] |
|-----|-----|-----|-----|
| **Nacht** | **nackt** | **Sachen** | **sacken** |
| **taucht** | **taugt** | **doch** | **Dock** |
| **pochen** | **Pocken** | | |

**ch** is soft [ç] after **ä**, **e**, **i**, **ei**, **ö**, **ü**, **eu**, **äu** and all consonants (everything else).

**Nächte** [nɛ çtɛ]     **Mächte** [mɛçtɛ]     **recht** [rɛçt]
**brecht** [brɛçt]     **Knecht** [knɛçt]     **nicht** [nIçt]
**spricht** [ʃprIçt]     **leicht** [lɑ:Içt]     **streichen** [ʃtrɑ:Içən]
**Töchter** [tœç tər]     **möchte** [mœç tɛ]     **Tücher** [ty çər]
**Früchte** [frYç tɛ]     **leuchten** [lɔ:yç tən]     **euch** [ɔ:yç]
**feucht** [fɔ:yçt]     **Gesträuche** [gɛ ʃtrɔ:yçɛ]
**räuchern** [rɔ:yçərn]     **durch** [dUrç]     **Storch** [ʃtɔrç]
**solche** [zɔlçɛ]     **Milch** [mIlç]     **manche** [mɑn çɛ]

Difficult words needing special attention:

**nichts** [nIçts]     **sprichst** [ʃprIçst]
**Störche** [ʃtœr çɛ]     **herrlichster** [hɛr:r lIç stər]
**Höchster** [høç stər]     **fürchte** [fYrç tɛ]
**schmeichelnd** [ʃmɑ:I çəlnt]     **schüchtern** [ʃYç tərn]

Under no circumstances should [ç] be confused with [ʃ].
**Doch wie! Täuscht mich nicht mein Ohr?**
**Er scheint mich noch nicht zu sehn.**
**Täuscht das Licht des Monds mich nicht... (Der Freischütz)**

chs
*Initial* **c** *and* **ch**
*in foreign words*

**chs** is pronounced [ks] when **s** is part of the root.

    **du wächst** [vɛkst] (from **wachsen**)

    **Dachs** [dɑks]    **Fuchs** [fUks]    **Ochs** [ɔks]

    **sechs** [zɛks]    **Wechsel** [vɛksəl]

Notice that **s** is not part of the root in

    **du weichst** [vɑ:Içst]    (from **weichen**)

    **du wachst** [vɑxst]    (from **wachen**)

    **des Dachs** [dɑxs]    (from **Dach**)

    **herrlichste** [hɛr:rlIçstɛ] (from **Herr**)

**c** standing by itself sometimes occurs at the beginnings of words which are non-German in origin. **z** is often substituted for **c**. In either spelling, the consonant sounds [ts].

    **Citrone** [tsi tro nɛ]    **Cäsar** [tse² zɑr]

    **Cypresse** [tsy prɛs:sɛ]    **Cäcilie** [tse² tsi ljɛ]

Initial **ch** in words not German in origin has a variety of pronunciations.

    [k]  **Chaos, Chloë, Choral, Christ, Chrysantemen**

    [ʃ]  **Chaconne, Charlotte**

    [x]  **Charkov**

    [tʃ]  English and Spanish words and names

    [ç]  **Cherubim, China**

**b**  is usually pronounced as in English (**bein, beben, Bube**) but is unvoiced when final, or when it comes at the end of a root-stem and is followed by a consonant.

**Laub** [lɑ:Up]    **lebt** [lept]    **Liebling** [liplIŋ]
**Lieb** [lip]    **gibt** [gipt]    **Grabgeläute** [grapgɛlɔ:ytɛ]

**ck**  is a double consonant. It is pronounced as a double **k**.

**Ecke** [ɛk:kɛ]    **stecken** [ʃtɛk:kən]
**Stück** [ʃtYk:k]    **Locken** [lɔk:kən]

**d**  is sharp and explosive, as in clear English.

**dir**    **Dunst**    **dein**

but is unvoiced when final, or when followed by another consonant at the end of a root-stem. See page 240.

**und**  [Unt]    **fand**  [fɑnt]    **Stand**  [ʃtɑnt]
**Bildnis** [bIltnIs]    **Mädchen** [me²t çən]    **Rundschau** [rUnt ʃɑ:u]

**dt**  in modern spelling is a double consonant equivalent to **tt**.

**Städtchen** [ʃtɛt:tçən]

Often **dt** occurring in pre 20th century texts is an old spelling and should be considered a single consonant.

old: **Todt** [tot]    new: **Tod** [tot]

**f**  as in English.

**fromm**  **finden**  **hoffen**  **Ofen**  **Waffe**  **offen**

*Consonants*
**g, ig, ng**

**g**   is usually pronounced [g].
**Grund**   **gegeben**   **General**

When final, it is pronounced [k] unless it follows **i** or **n**.
**Tag**   **Weg**   **weg**   **sagt**   **verbirg**

**ng**   Siebs cautions against unvoicing a final **g** when it is preceded by **n**.
**bang** [baŋ] *not* [baŋk]    **sing** [zIŋ] *not* [zIŋk]

final **ig**   is pronounced [Iç]
**König**   **wenig**   **ewig**   **selig**

otherwise **ig**   is pronounced [Iç] when it ends a root and is followed by a consonant.
**Ewigkeit**   **Seligkeit**   **freudigste**

**ig** is pronounced [Ik] when it is followed by the suffixes **-lich** or **-reich**.   **ewiglich**   **Königreich**

**grimmig** [grIm:mIç]    **grimmigen** [grIm:mIgən]
**grimmigste** [grIm:mIçstɛ]    **grimmiglich** [grIm:mIklIç]

*Consonants*
**h, k, l, m**

**h** is pronounced   as in English
        1   when it begins a word.
            **Hauch     holen     Hausherr**

        2   when it begins a root.
            **verhalten     Gehalt     erhebt     Haushofmeister**

        3   when it occurs in short exclamations.
            **oho     aha**

        4   when it begins the suffixes -**heit** and -**haft**.
            **Schönheit     lebhaft**

**h** is silent   in all other cases.
            **ihr     sehen     ruhig**

**k**   is pronounced as in English.
        **Kunst     Kirche     Ek-ke     Brük-ke**

**l**   is forward and dental.
        **lau     alte     mild     Wellen     alle     gefallen**

**m**   is pronounced as in English. It must have pitch.
        **mild     Mime     manche     Himmel     Kummer     summen**

**n**    is dental and is therefore more resonant than in English.
**nein  Sinn  nennen  kennen  sehen  gehen  geben**

**ng**    is pronounced [ŋ] as in English **sing** or **singer**. The **g** never sounds separately. German **ng** always sounds as in **Long Island**, never as in **Long Guy-land** or **finger**.
**bang** [baŋ]  **bangen** [baŋən]  **Engel** [ɛŋəl]  **fangen** [faŋən]
**lang** [laŋ]  **länger** [lɛŋər]  **Angel** [aŋəl]  **Wangen** [vaŋən]

Siebs advises against unvoicing final **ng**. See page 245.

**nk**    is pronounced [ŋk], as in English **rink** [rɪŋk].
**danken    Funken    schlanke    kranken**

**p**    is pronounced explosively as in English.
**Pein    packen    Perle    Lippen    Sippe    Pfund**
**Pferd    Pfeil    Pfitzner    pflangen    Wappen**

**ph**    is equivalent to [f].
**Phantasie** [fan ta zi]

**qu**    is pronounced [kv].
**Qual** [kval]    **Quelle**    [kvɛl:lɛ]
**quer** [kver]    **erquicken** [ɛr kvɪk:kən]

Although uvular **r** is widely used in German speech, it is not used
in singing. Likewise, in the spoken language **r** may be dropped when
it is final or when it comes before another consonant, but not in
the sung language. In stage diction **r** must always be pronounced,
either flipped or trilled, according to the circumstances.

**r** between vowels   should get only a single flip.
                   **ihre**      **Ohren**

final **r**   should not be trilled but may receive a single or double flip—enough
                   to make it audible.

**r** otherwise   may be trilled for emphasis, if appropriate to the context.

| | | | |
|---|---|---|---|
| **reichste** | **reizend** | **traurig** | **rauschen** |
| **brechen** | **fröhlich** | **froh** | **zürnen** |

**rr**   double **r** should be trilled.

| | |
|---|---|
| **irre** | **knurren** |

*Consonants*
**s**

initial **s**    in word or root is voiced [z].
        **sagen** [zɑ gǝn]    **Seele** [ze lɛ]    **suche** [zu xɛ]    **ansagen** [ɑn zɑ gǝn]

final **s**    is unvoiced [s].
        **Haus** [hɑ:Us]    **als** [ɑls]    **uns** [Uns]    **lösbar** [løs bɑr]

**s** between vowels    is voiced [z].
        **Rose** [ro zɛ]    **Rasen** [rɑ zǝn]    **böse** [bø zɛ]
        **erlösen** [ɛr lø zǝn]    **Wesen** [ve zǝn]

genitive **s**    between two parts of a compound is unvoiced.
        **Lebensreise** [le bǝns rɑ:Izɛ]    **Himmelsblau** [hIm:mǝls blɑ:U]

interior **s**

1    preceded by a voiced consonant and followed by a vowel, is voiced [z]. This may be conveniently remembered as the "Unser Rule".
        **unser** [Un zǝr]    **also** [ɑl zo]    **Amsel** [ɑm zǝl]
        **winseln** [vIn zǝln]    **Ferse** [fɛr zɛ]

2    in the suffixes **-sal** and **-sam** is voiced.
        **Schicksal** [ʃIk:k zɑl]    **seltsam** [zɛlt zɑm]

3    Otherwise, **s** interior is unvoiced.
        **Fenster**    **lispeln**    **Wespe**

Summary    **s** is voiced 1 when initial in word or root.    **Sonne**
                    2 when intervocalic.    **Rose**
                    3 the **Unser** Rule.    **unser**
                    4 the suffixes **-sal**, **-sam**.    **Schicksal, seltsam**

        **s** is unvoiced in all other cases.

**sch**    is pronounced [ʃ].
     **Schatten    schön    schon    rasch    Schmetterling**

**sp**    is pronounced [ʃp] when it occurs at the beginning of a word or root-stem.
     **Spass**      [ʃpɑs:s]         **Spott**      [ʃpɔt:t]      **springen** [ʃprI ŋən
     **gesprungen** [gɛ ʃprU ŋən]      **Kinderspiel** [kIn dər ʃpil]

But in words like **Wespe, lispeln,** etc., the **s** sounds as [s] because it is not at the beginning of a root-stem.

**ss**    is unvoiced and prolonged [s:s]. For the spelling see page 225.
     **wissen** [vIs:sən]      **süsse**    [zys:sɛ]      **hassen** [hɑs:sən]
     **Messer** [mɛs:sər]      **küssen** [kYs:sən]

**st**    is pronounced [ʃt] when it occurs at the beginning of a word or root-stem.
     **stehen**      [ʃte ən]      **Stunde**    [ʃtUn dɛ]      **stolz** [ʃtɔlts]
     **gestanden** [gɛ ʃtɑn dən]      **verstehen** [fɛr ʃte ən]
     **Feuerstrahl** [fɔ:yər ʃtrɑl]

But in words like **finster, gestern, Fenster, Hofmannsthal,** etc., the **s** sounds as [s] because it is not at the beginning of a root-stem.

**t**   is sharp and explosive, as in clear British English.
**tun  Takt  Lust  fest  Blätter  Schatten  fetter**

**ti**   is occasionally found in loan-words and is sounded [ts].
**Nation** [nɑ tsjon]   **Station** [ʃtɑ tsjon]

**th**   is the same as **t**. See page 225.
**Thal = Tal   Thau = Tau   thun = tun**

**tsch**   [tʃ] is equivalent to the initial sound in English **choose**.
**plätschert** [plɛ tʃərt]  **zwitschert** [tsvI tʃərt]  **Deutsch** [dɔ:ytʃ]

**tz**   is pronounced as a double consonant [t:s]. Its sound is similar to
**zz** in Italian words such as **pezzo, pizza.**
| | | | |
|---|---|---|---|
| **sitzen** | [zIt:sən] | **setzen** | [zɛt:sən] |
| **letzten** | [lɛt:s tən] | **kratzen** | [krɑt:sən] |
| **Spitz** | [ʃpIt:s] | **Fritz** | [frIt:s] |

**v**   is pronounced [f].
**Vater  vergehen  Vogel  von  vor**

Exception   in words of foreign derivation: sometimes [v].
**Vase  Rosenkavalier  Nachtviolen**

**w**   is pronounced [v].
**Wagner  weg  Weg  Wange  wohin**

**x**   is pronounced [ks]. **Axis**

**z**   is pronounced [ts].
**Zier** [tsir]  **Zähne** [tse² nɛ]  **Zug** [tsuk]
**zusammen** [tsu zɑm:mən]  **zwischen** [tsvI ʃən]

*Elision*

It is incorrect to elide into a German word or root which begins with a vowel. Although vocal legato may be enhanced by such elision, it is stylistically incorrect.

**die /Ehre    über /ihn    Der /Alte    ver/achten    ge/ahnt**

In order to avoid a merciless chopping of the vocal line, minimize the amount of separation between these words, lengthening the syllable (i.e., the vowel) before the separation as much as possible. To find a parallel in English, try singing the words **your eyes** as smoothly linked together as possible, without letting the phrase sound like **your rise**.

Sometimes a noticable break between words can even bring out the meaning of the word. In **Ich bin allein**, for example, a healthy amount of separation between the second and third words will give **allein** much more significance.

A word ending in a consonant should be smoothly linked to a word beginning with a consonant. Singers striving for clarity sometimes unwittingly insert neutral vowels between words.

**in—uh—dem    Länger trag ich—uh—nicht—uh—die Qualen**
**Und ewig wäre sie dann—uh—mein**

Such insertions are confusing. They do nothing to improve clarity and usually are indications that vowels are not being sustained to their proper length.

In the succession **in dem**, for example, the **i** of the first word should be held as long as possible. The singer should not let go of the **n** until he has begun to articulate the **d** of **dem**.

The only elision in German occurs in compound adverbs (**herauf**, **hinaus**, etc.). In them, the final consonant of the first part of the compound must elide into the vowel beginning the second root. In no other case is elision made in German, either between words or even between parts of a compound word.

If you are told that "your German does not sound very German", go over the following check-list of common errors made by American singers.

1 *Are the high vowels high enough? Are the round vowels round enough?* The answer is often no to both questions.

2 *Do you slide into vowels?* Formation of the vowel simultaneously with the consonant preceding it will correct the fault.

3 *Do you maintain the same vowel quality throughout the length of the vowel sound?* Use a mirror to help you check. Lips, tongue and jaw should not move while a vowel is being sustained. If they do, the vowel quality will change, and you will have an unwanted diphthong. Anticipation of a following consonant is usually the reason for a change in vowel quality or even vowel identity.

4 *Are you articulating all consonants?* Americans are always trying to simplify pronunciation by omitting and/or imploding consonants, especially when they occur in clusters. We do it all the time in English. If it is done in German, an important element of the flavor of the language is lost. In **Du bist die Ruh'**, the **t** of **bist** must be clearly articulated just before the **d** of **die**.

5 *Are you correct in your use of* [x] *and* [ç] *for German* **ch?** Is your [ç] too far back and therefore weak in projection? Is your [ç] too similar in sound to [ʃ]? (Does it sound "ishy"? ) Review exercises 75 and 76 in Part 1, relating to [ç], [ʃ] and [x].

6 *Do you elide into words or roots beginning with a vowel?* This is **verboten**.

# ADDITIONAL BIBLIOGRAPHY

| | | | |
|---|---|---|---|
| **Adler, Kurt** | 1965 | The Art of Accompanying and Coaching | Minneapolis: The University of Minnesota Press |
| **Agard and Di Pietro** | 1965 | The Sounds of English and Italian | Chicago: The University of Chicago Press |
| **Bernac, Pierre** | 1970 | The Interpretation of French Song | New York: Praeger Publishers |
| **Colorni, Evelina** | 1970 | Singers' Italian | New York: G. Schirmer |
| **Coscia, Silvio** | 1969 | Operative Italian Diction and Articulation Applied to Singing | Boston: The New England Conservatory |
| **Cox, Richard G.** | 1970 | The Singer's Manual of German and French Diction | New York: G. Schirmer |
| **Demers, Jeanne** | 1962 | Phonétique théorique et pratique | Montréal: Editions Centre de Psychologie et de Pédagogie |
| **Errolle, Ralphe** | 1963 | Italian Diction for Singers | Boulder, Colorado: Pruett Press, Inc. |
| **Grammont, Maurice** | 1963 | La prononciation française | Paris: Librairie Delagrave |
| **Hogben, Lancelot** | 1965 | The Mother Tongue | New York: W. W. Norton & Co. |

| | | | |
|---|---|---|---|
| **International Phonetic Assn.** | 1961 | The Principles of the International Phonetic Association | London: University College |
| **Marshall, Madeleine** | 1953 | The Singer's Manual of English Diction | New York: G. Schirmer |
| **Martinet, André** | 1966 | Elements of General Linguistics | Chicago: University of Chicago Press |
| **Martinon, Ph.** | 1913 | Comment on prononce le français | Paris: Librairie Larousse |
| **Migliorini, Bruno** | 1964 | La lingua italiana d'oggi | Torino: Edizioni RAI Radio-televisione italiana |
| **Moulton, William G.** | 1962 | The Sounds of German and English | Chicago: The University of Chicago Press |
| **Pei, Mario** | 1954 | The Italian Language | New York: S. F. Vanni |
| **Peyrollaz and Tovar** | 1954 | Manuel de phonétique et de diction françaises | Paris: Librairie Larousse |
| **Posner, Rebecca** | 1966 | The Romance Languages | Garden City, N.Y.: Doubleday & Co., Inc. |
| **Rebora, Piero** | 1964 | Cassell's Italian-English Dictionary | New York: Funk & Wagnall's |
| **Russo, Joseph Louis** | 1947 | Present Day Italian | Boston: D. C. Heath & Co. |
| **Sturtevant, E. H.** | 1965 | Linguistic Change | Chicago: University of Chicago Press |
| **Turgeon, Frederick King** | 1947 | Cours pratique de français | New York: D. Appleton-Century Co., Inc. |

# Index of sounds

| Page number in Part 1 | | Vowels (Exercise numbers are in bold face) | | |
|---|---|---|---|---|
| | | English | Italian | Latin |
| 9 25-27 | [i] | meet, key | chi 115 **15** | Filio 155 |
| 11 27 | [e] | — | — | — |
| 9 29 | [I] | mitt, hit | — | — |
| 11 31 | [e²] | chaotic | vero 116-120 126-128 **22** | — |
| 9 33 | [ɛ] | bed | bello 116-120 126-128 **23** | requiem 155 |
| 61 | [ɛ̃] | — | — | — |
| 11 33 | [a] | — | — | — |
| 15 47 | [ɑ] | father | alma 115 **33** | mala 155 |
| 59 | [ɑ̃] | — | — | — |
| 13 47 | [ɔ] | jaw | morte 116-117 122-128 **32** | Domine 156 |
| 15 45 | [o²] | rowing | nome, dolce 116-117 122-128 **31** | — |
| 13 43 | [U] | foot | — | — |
| 15 39-41 | [o] | — | — | — |
| 63 | [õ] | — | — | — |
| 13 35-37 | [u] | moon | luna 115 **25** | unum 156 |
| 19 49 | [y] | — | — | — |
| 19 53-55 | [Y] | — | — | — |
| 19 51 55 | [ø] | — | — | — |
| 19 57 | [œ] | — | — | — |
| 63 | [œ̃] | — | — | — |
| 21-23 | [ə] | Rita, oven | — | — |
| | [ɛ̃] | — | — | — |
| 33 | [æ] | cat | — | — |
| 19 | [3] | first | — | — |
| 23 | [ʌ] | cup | — | — |

| French | German |
|---|---|
| qui, cygne 177 **15 17 35** | liebe, ihn, wir 225-227 231-232 **16 20** |
| parlé, nez, parler, parlerai 180-183 **17 18** | Seele, geben, Weh 226-227 231 233 **16 18 21 36** |
| — | mit, sitzen 225-226 228 234 **39** |
| — | Tränen 226-227 232-233 **21 22** |
| belle, avait, mai, tête | Bett, hätte 225-226 228 234 **21 23 42** |
| seine 180-183 **23 49** | |
| sein, pain, fin, faim, thym 189-190 **49 50** | — |
| voilà la salade 175 194 | — |
| âme 176 194 **33 45** | Vater, Mahler 226 **33** |
| enfant, champ, Jean, paon 189 **45 46 47 48** | — |
| sortir, aura 184 **32** | Dorn 226 228 233-235 **32 42** |
| — | — |
| — | Mutter 225-226 228 233-235 **29 30 39** |
| rose, ôter, pot, beau, faut, écho 184 **26 27 36 51** | Rose, tot, froh 226-227 232-233 235 **26 27 36** |
| fond, ombre 190 **51 52** | — |
| fou 177 **24 25 27** | Uhr, Buch, tun 225-227 232-233 235 **24 27 30** |
| tu, flûte, eût 187 **34 35** | früh, Tür 225-227 232-233 235 **34 35 41** |
| — | Glück 225-226 228 233-235 **39 40 41** |
| peu, berceuse 186 **36 37 44** | schön 226-227 232-233 235 **37 41 44** |
| coeur, fleur 186 **42 43 44 56** | können 226 228 231 234-235 **42 43 44** |
| parfum, défunt 190 **53** | — |
| je, faisant, parlent *(forward-use lips)* 178 | lieben 229 |
| — | Liebe 229 |
| — | — |
| — | — |
| — | — |

| Page number in Part 1 | Glides, Diphthongs and Triphthongs (Exercise numbers are in bold face) | | | |
|---|---|---|---|---|
| | | English | Italian | Latin |
| 73 | [j] | yes *(no buzz)* | **ieri** *(no buzz)* 131-134 **61** | **ejus** *(no buzz)* 158 |
| 75 | [w] | west | **guarda** 131-134 **62** | **qui, linguis** 158 |
| 75 | [ɥ] | — | — | — |
| 75 | [ʎ] | lute | **gl'occhi** 131-134 **64** | — |
| 67 | [ɑːi] | mine, high | **mai** 129 134 **54** | **Laicus** 157 |
| 67 | [ɑːI] | mine, high | — | — |
| 67 | [aj] | — | — | — |
| 67 | [ɛːi] | say, mate | **sei** 129-134 **55** | **mei** 157 |
| 67 | [ɛːI] | say, mate | — | — |
| 67 | [ɛj] | — | — | — |
| 69 | [œj] | — | — | — |
| 69 | [uj] | — | — | — |
| 69 | [oːu] | grow | — | — |
| 69 | [ɔːi] | boy | **poi** 129-134 **58** | — |
| 69 | [ɔːI] | boy | — | — |
| 69 | [ɔːy] | — | — | — |
| 71 | [ɑːu] | cow | **aura** 129-134 **59** | **laudamus** 157 |
| 71 | [ɑːU] | cow | — | — |
| 71 | [ɑːo] | — | — | — |
| | [ɛːə] | air | — | — |
| | [Iːə] | ear | — | — |
| | [ɔːə] | ore | — | — |
| | [Uːə] | sure | — | — |
| | [ɑːiə] | fire | — | — |
| | [ɑːuə] | our | — | — |
| | [ɔːyə] | — | — | — |

*Consonants: Plosives*

| | | English | Italian | Latin |
|---|---|---|---|---|
| 81 | [p] | **pepper** *(explosive)* | **papa** *(dry)* 138 142 **67 68** | **peccata** *(dry)* 159 |
| 81 | [b] | **bow** | **bada** 138 142 | **beata** 159 |
| 83 | [t] | **tent** *(sharp, alveolar)* | **tutto** *(dry, dental)* 138 142 **69 70** | **terra, catholicam** *(dry, dental)* 161 |
| 83 | [d] | **dead** *(alveolar)* | **doppio** *(dental)* 138 142 **69** | **Domine** *(dental)* 159 |
| 85 | [k] | **cat, chorus, quick** *(explosive)* | **come, ecco, chioma, che questo** *(dry)* 140 149 **71 72** | **credo, bracchio** *(dry)* **mihi** 160-161 |
| 85 | [g] | **give** | **gamba, grande, gonfia** 140 **72** | **gaudebit** 160 |

| French | German |
|---|---|
| **bien, moyen** 189 195-196 **61** | **Jahr** 237 **60** |
| **oui** 194 196 **62** | — |
| **nuit** 187 193 196 **63** | — |
| — | — |
| — | — |
| — | **mein, Hain** 237 **54** |
| **corail** 195 **54** | — |
| — | — |
| — | — |
| **soleil** 181 195 **55** | — |
| **deuil** 186 195 **56** | — |
| **fenouil** 195 **57** | — |
| — | — |
| — | — |
| — | — |
| — | **treu, träumen** 237 **58** |
| — | — |
| — | **Tau** 237 **59** |
| — | **Tau** 237 **59** |
| — | — |
| — | — |
| — | — |
| — | — |
| — | — |
| — | — |
| — | **Feuer** 237 |

| French | German |
|---|---|
| **papa, absent** *(dry)* 199 203 **67 68** | **Paar, lieb** *(explosive)* 247 **66** |
| **bas** 198 203 | **Bett** 240 244 |
| **tantot** *(dry, dental, palatalized before* [i] [y] [j] [ɥ]*)* **tire, tu, tiens, tuer** 202 204 **69 70** | **Tante, Grund, Thau** *(sharp, alveolar)* 225 244 251 **69** |
| **dindon** *(dental; palatalized before* [i] [y] [j] [ɥ]*)* **dire, dure, Dieu, réduit** 199 204 **69** | **decken** *(alveolar)* 244 **69** |
| **comment, qui, choeur** *(dry, except before* [i] [y] [j] [ɥ]*)* 205 **71 72** | **Kunst, Qual, Chor, Tag** *(explosive)* 240 242-245 247 |
| **gauche, grande** 205 **72** | **geben, General** 245 |

| Page number in Part 1 | | Consonants: Fricatives (Exercise numbers are in bold face) | | |
| --- | --- | --- | --- | --- |
| | | *English* | *Italian* | *Latin* |
| 87 | [f] | father, physic | fuori 146 **73** | fecit 159 |
| 87 | [v] | visit | vecchio, Wanda 149 **73** | vestrum 159 |
| 87-89 | [ʃ] | shine *(bright)* | lascia *(bright)* 141 **74** | scitote 161 |
| 87 | [ʒ] | Asia *(bright)* | — | — |
| 89 | [s] | simple, receive | seno, questo 143-144 | salutare 161 |
| 89 | [z] | roses, zoo | rosa, sdegno 143-144 | — |
| | [θ] | three | — | — |
| | [ð] | this | vado | — |
| 89 | [ç] | human | — | — |
| 91 | [x] | — | — | — |
| 91 | [h] | house, who | — | — |
| | | *Consonants: Nasals* | | |
| 93 | [m] | mother | mamma 138-139 147 | mortuus 159 |
| 93 | [n] | nose | naso 138-139 147 | nescio 159 |
| 77 | [ɲ] | onion | ognuno 149 **65** | agnus 160 |
| 95 | [ŋ] | ring, thank | sangue, anche 149 **77** | — |
| | | *Consonants: Lateral and Trilled* | | |
| 97 | [l] | liquid | largo, alto 138-139 146 **78** | alleluia 159 |
| | [ɫ] | milk | — | — |
| 99 | [r] | three | rosa, orrore 148 **80** | rex 159 |

*(flipped or trilled in singing all four languages, except that English*

| | | *Consonants: Affricates* | | |
| --- | --- | --- | --- | --- |
| 101 | [tʃ] | cheer, pitch | cielo, cenere 131 141 | cibo, coelo, caeca 160 |
| 101 | [dʒ] | joy, George | gioia, gemo 131 141 | pange, regina 160 |
| 101 | [ts] | cats | zio, senza 138-139 145 **81** | gratias, justitia 161 |
| 101 | [dz] | leads | azzuro, bonzo 138-139 145 148 **81** | azymis 162 |

| *French* | *German* |
|---|---|
| **fou, phare** 199 204 **73** | **Vater, Phantasie** 244 247 251 **73** |
| **vent, wagon** 204 **73** | **Weg** 251 **73** |
| **charme** *(dark)* 205 **74** | **schön, Stadt, Spass** *(dark)* 250 **74 75** |
| **je, givre** *(dark)* 205 **74** | — |
| **soixante, cent, leçon, jasmin** 207-208 | **essen, Fenster, Haus** 225 235 238 249-250 |
| **rose, azure** 208 | **Seele, unser, Rose** 249 |
| — | — |
| — | — |
| — | **ich, recht** 242 **75 76** |
| — | **Nacht, doch, such** 242 **76** |
| — | **Haus, lebhaft** 246 |
| **maman** 206 | **Mutter, nahm** 238-239 246 |
| **nez** 206 | **nein, Nase** *(dental)* 238-239 247 |
| **oignon, agneau** 206 **65** | — |
| — | **Ring, Dank** 245 247 |
| **large, fatal** 199 206 **78** | **links, alte, also** 238-239 246 **78** |
| — | — |
| **roucoule** 200 206 **79 80** | **Retter, irre** 238-239 248 **79 80** |

*may also use the American r for a more informal style)*

| | |
|---|---|
| — | **plätschert** 251 |
| — | — |
| — | **Zimmer, Spitz** 251 **81** |
| — | — |